W9-DBD-676

The Public Relations Firm

Humber College Library
3199 Lakeshore Blvd. West
Toronto, ON   M8V 1K8

The Public Relations Firm

Bob "Pritch" Pritchard, APR, Fellow PRSA,
Captain, U.S. Navy (Ret.)
Stacey Smith, APR, Fellow PRSA

HUMBER LIBRARIES LAKESHORE CAMPUS
3199 Lakeshore Blvd West
TORONTO, ON.   M8V 1K8

DISCARD

 BUSINESS EXPERT PRESS

The Public Relations Firm
Copyright © Business Expert Press, LLC, 2015.

All rights reserved. No part of this publication may be reproduced, stored in a retrieval system, or transmitted in any form or by any means—electronic, mechanical, photocopy, recording, or any other except for brief quotations, not to exceed 400 words, without the prior permission of the publisher.

First published in 2015 by
Business Expert Press, LLC
222 East 46th Street, New York, NY 10017
www.businessexpertpress.com

ISBN-13: 978-1-60649-664-0 (paperback)
ISBN-13: 978-1-60649-665-7 (e-book)

Business Expert Press Public Relations Collection

Collection ISSN: 2157-345X (print)
Collection ISSN: 2157-3476 (electronic)

Cover and interior design by S4Carlisle Publishing Services Private Ltd., Chennai, India

First edition: 2015

10 9 8 7 6 5 4 3 2 1

Printed in the United States of America

Dedication

This book is dedicated to my mom, Shirley Smith, who taught me that if you really love what you do then a job isn't work at all, and to my JJ&W colleagues who made all these years so much fun!

Stacey Smith, APR, Fellow PRSA
Senior Counsel & Partner
Jackson Jackson & Wagner

I dedicate this book to my father, who passed before he could see the final result. He was a great man and one of my greatest supporters and advisers. I hope I made you proud, dad! I also want to thank my wife of 20 years, Brenda Gayle, for her support and encouragement.

Bob "Pritch" Pritchard, APR, Fellow PRSA
Captain, U.S. Navy (Ret.)
Instructor & Faculty Adviser, Lindsey + Asp

Abstract

This book takes an in-depth look at the client/agency relationship by discussing what business leaders should expect of their public relations firms. It discusses *how* and *why* they should pick an agency along with the types of firms at their disposal. The business of public relations is covered in the first section of the book. The second section provides detail on the relationship between firm and client and focuses on what firms must do to satisfy client expectations of their work. The third and final section outlines how firms establish success or failure. Expert advice is provided on everything from hiring a firm to defining output and outcome expectations and everything in between.

Keywords

PR firms; PR agencies; Hiring a PR firm (agency); How to Hire a Public Relations (pr) firm (agency); Hiring a pr (public relations) firm (agency) (company) (person); How PR firm's bill; Evaluating a pr firm (agency) (plan) (campaign); PR firm billing rates; pr firm (agency) contracts ; pr practitioner roles, Responsibilities; Public relations evaluation; Client-Firm relationship; Public relations research; Public relations execution

Table of Contents

Preface ....*xi*

Introduction 1

Part I   **The Business**... 3

Chapter 1   Why Hire a Public Relations Firm? 5

Chapter 2   Types of Firms...17

Chapter 3   Hiring a Firm...27

Chapter 4   Defining the Work 35

Chapter 5   How Firms Bill 45

Part II   **The Working Relationship between**
               Client and Firm... 57

Chapter 6   The Client–Firm Relationship 59

Chapter 7   Progress Reports..69

Chapter 8   Research and Execution.....................................77

Chapter 9   Evaluation 87

Part III   **Meeting Expectations: Measurement**
               and Evaluation... 93

Chapter 10   Meeting Client Expectations 95

Chapter 11   Wrapping Up 103

References..*107*

Index *109*

Preface

My coauthor and I were asked to collaborate on this book by our editor, Don Stacks. Don is one of the top researchers in public relations, especially in measurement and evaluation. He's also been my mentor since I first entered academe in the fall of 2001, so it was a tremendous honor to be asked by him to write a book.

This is my first book, though I had contributed several chapters to other texts. Stacey Smith, my coauthor, had the edge on me as she's coauthored one of the top case study textbooks and edited and wrote for the well-thought-of industry publication *pr reporter* for more than 20 years. Still, the challenge was a little daunting for us both.

When Stacey and I first sat down to organize this book, we had in mind practicing business executives. It has always been our hope that this book will help inform management practice and help current and future business leaders identify and better utilize public relations firms and independent professionals.

But, we also knew the audience was broader than that. We hope this volume is helpful to students and faculty in any number of public relations classes, including Introduction to Public Relations. And while a niche market, we hope our book will be especially helpful to students and faculty starting or growing a student-run public relations firm. As these experiential learning laboratories have become more popular, the need for information on the business side of agency operations is more in evidence than ever.

We start our book with an in-depth look at the client/agency relationship, discussing what business leaders should expect of their public relations firms. We discuss *how* and *why* they should pick an agency along with the types of firms at their disposal. The business of public relations is covered in the first section of the book. The second section provides detail on the relationship between firm and client and focuses on what firms must do to satisfy client expectations of their work. The third and final section outlines how firms establish success or failure.

While we met and overcame significant challenges during spring 2014, the process of writing this book has been a real pleasure and learning experience for Stacey and me. As you will read in our bios, I'm deeply involved with student-run public relations firms and Stacey is Senior Counsel and Partner at one of the top behavioral public relations and management consulting firms in the country. Even with that experience we are better professionals for this journey, giving us a more global and well-rounded knowledge of firm operations.

We would be remiss if we failed to acknowledge the help and support of our editor, our families, and our colleagues in writing this book. A special "Thank you" goes out to Peter Debreceny and Ron Culp, who reviewed our second round edits and provided exceptionally insightful comments. And, of course, we want to give a special acknowledgment to our editor, Don Stacks. Without his expert guidance and patience this book might well have ended up on Jimmy Fallon's "Do not read" list.

Introduction

Why do organizations decide to hire outside public relations counsel? What drives them to this decision and how, with so many competitors vying for their attention and their business, do they find the right match in terms of skills, people power, budget, and work style? How will they measure the success of the relationship?

Public relations agencies/firms are ubiquitous in many ways, meaning there are a lot of choices to be considered from a friend or a family member who "does PR" to small firms, large agencies, and independent practitioners. Typically, the organization seeking counsel makes a determination based on their own perception of need for various skills, depth of experience, extra hands, or industry understanding.

The organization issue that needs addressing might be in the arena of public policy; therefore, an agency with lobbying and political experience is needed. Or it might be in the arena of sales support; thus the need is for skills in marketing and sales promotion and publicity. Or needs may require organizational development skills, which would call for an agency that understands internal communication, facilitation, and organization development. However, the tasks the organization thinks they want to address may be only symptoms of a different, more complex issue needing an entirely different approach or set of skills.

Where should an organization start? What are the questions they should ask? What are some realistic expectations? These are the underlying issues this book seeks to address. If an organization is considering hiring an agency/firm to assist, starting with this book will make that relationship and its outcomes all the more successful.

Stacey Smith
Rye, NH
Robert "Pritch" Pritchard
Norman, OK

Note: It is the preference of these authors to refer to "agencies" as "firms" in general and in this book. Some say the term "agency" suggests that counsel is in a vendor relationship, offering a product that is interchangeable with others offering the same product. Others say the term implies the firm is acting as an agent of the client, which captures a singular task such as speaking to the media on the client's behalf, for example.

Public Relations has been referred to over the past several decades as both a science and an art (www.instituteforpr.org). Like an organization's relationship with its attorneys, the professional services we offer clients are not a "product," but counsel. And today, public relations encompasses much more than just media relations. Therefore the authors prefer (and will use herein) the term "firm" in place of "agency." We urge you to consider this semantics nuance when you seek your next relationship with a public relations firm. We also prefer to use the term "public relations" rather than its sometimes pejorative abbreviation "PR." An entity that approaches your organization and its issues like a vendor will provide a very different and a much shallower and less effective manner from a firm.

PART I

The Business

Many consider public relations a part of the promotional trinity: Advertising, Marketing, and Public Relations, sometimes called the "3 Ps": Publicity, Product, Promotion. In actuality, all three have something in common, but also have a great many differences. To begin with, public relations deals with *two-way symmetrical* communication (Grunig and Hunt 1984)—where messages are communicated with the purpose of achieving a dialogue between an organization, brand, issue, and specified target audiences or public. Although often put at the end of the promotional process, public relations is vital when trying to influence people to do or purchase something. Today, this is even more important as we find more and more promotional messages being transmitted through social media, a media that encourages two-way symmetrical communication.

Second, while public relations continues to have its "artsy" side—that is the creation of well-written and graphically designed communication materials—it is also heavily influenced by the social sciences and even the natural sciences. This is especially true when the objective of the public relations campaign or program is to influence an audience. The underlying strategy (theory) in many cases is attitude change that results in some behavior change (Bowen et al. 2010; Michaelson and Stacks 2014). Indeed, Michaelson and Stacks (2014, p. 25) propose a model of public relations in the following graphic, where the message is first evaluated and then moved from objective to objective, depending on the stage of the BASIC life cycle.

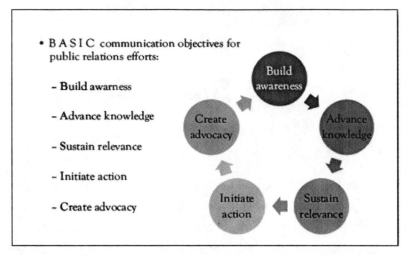

Figure I.1 The communication life cycle

This model requires that research be conducted on the problem at hand before a strategy or campaign can be conducted and it relies heavily on social scientific research on the influence process. It is an example of what the Institute for Public Relations (www.instituteforpr.org) calls the "science beneath the art."

But the most important aspect of the difference between public relations and advertising or marketing is that public relations is the business of change, reinforcing current beliefs, or inducing resistance to change, and its outcomes can be measured in terms of how returns on expectations (ROE) influence returns on investment (ROI) (Stacks 2011). The public relations effort has to begin with an established baseline, with set objectives that mirror the client's goals, and then demonstrate effectiveness by correlating success to other business functions (e.g., marketing, human resources, and finance) in driving toward meeting the business' goal. This book explores how that is done by outside consultants ("counsels") who are hired by the client to influence the behaviors of targeted audiences. Part I sets the basics.

CHAPTER 1

Why Hire a Public Relations Firm?

"The media and our opponents were bearing down through the news media and our leadership team kept fanning the flames, with no clue how to back off and resolve the issues. I had done all I could—they needed to hear from a different voice"
—Director of Communications, Government Entity

"We needed to have some concrete, objective data on what employees were thinking and needing in terms of communication systems"
—Director of Communications, Major Airline

"I had just taken over as head of the organization—I needed a candid assessment of the organization's relationships"
—Superintendent, Public/Private School

"We were having trouble reaching customers with our messaging. Either we were using the wrong channels or the wrong messages!"
—Executive Director, Non-Profit Organization

"My department was lean—too lean and we needed some extra hands that I couldn't afford to hire full time—to get the launch done"
—Director of Public Relations at a large manufacturing company

As we noted in the Introduction, there are a myriad of reasons organizations hire outside public relations firms. **Tactical reasons** can include:

- Needing skill sets that are not currently resident in the department
- Needing extra hands to handle a project, temporary or otherwise
- Seeking a wider range of creative thinking
- Making use of a firm's relationships/contacts with traditional and social media

Strategic reasons are broader and higher level. They can include:

- Experience with significant problems or opportunities that the organization may be facing including strategic planning, crises, reputational issues
- Building credibility for role and function of public relations with senior management or Board of organization
- Evaluation of staff, organizational structure, department structure, and effectiveness
- Research expertise with stakeholder groups to identify perceptions, attitudes, and behaviors along with effective methods of communication

So the question one must ask is *what actual needs does the organization have and what type of public relations firm is best to help fill those needs?*

Evaluating Your Needs

This is a bit like deciding you have a hip problem and going to an orthopedist for help. What if the problem is not the hip? What if it is muscular or a bad mattress? Will the orthopedist see only skeletal solutions? Did you need the expert first or the generalist to help you evaluate what is necessary?

Hiring the right public relations firm means *diagnosing the right problem.* Now a crisis where "60 Minutes" is knocking at your door or the entirety of local media is camped in your parking lot is pretty indicative that you need some help. Even a shortage of staffing is pretty self-evident. There is work to be done and not enough people to do it—so hiring "extra hands" is obvious. But is it? Have you identified the core problem, or just a symptom of a bigger problem that should be addressed? If customer satisfaction levels are down it could be that systems are not working well, but what if staff morale is down as well and causing a domino effect? Or, perhaps your communication staff is spending their time on activities that are more "make-work" than advancing the relationships that the organization actually needs. Much like zero-based budgeting, every public relations function should have a Strategic Plan that addresses all critical audiences.

Unless it is a crisis of major proportions, the best place to initially determine the type of firm you may need is the corporate communications department's Strategic Plan.[1] Make sure to have clear goals, objectives, and strategies based on the goals and objectives for the organization as whole for all priority audiences.[2] And if not, then this may be your *first skill set to consider* when hiring a public relations firm.

Key Elements to Look For in a Strategic Plan

There is a great difference between a general plan and one that is *strategic*. A strategic plan first and foremost has *public relations goals* that are directly related to the business goals and objectives of the organization as a whole. They should seek to further the ability of the organization to succeed by *targeting priority audiences* (customer, clients, employees, community, shareholder, and so forth) critical to making organizational goals achievable. Each of these priority *audiences* should have *targeted, measureable goals* for the time period of the plan. There should be a *strategy* on how to achieve the goals taking into account the possible barriers—both structural and psychological—to reaching those goals. Then the tactics

---

[1]For a more on the importance and role of the organization's communication strategy see Bowen, Rawlins, and Martin (2010), p. 26.
[2]For a more on understanding and measuring public relations outcomes see Michaelson and Stacks (2014), pp. 35–47.

should include *one-way, two-way* and *interpersonal communication tactics* because research has proven that behavior is motivated by not just by information but *relationships* (Deci and Ryan, 2000, p. 71). Finally, there should be some type of *measurement* in the plan that can give leadership a sense of whether the strategy, tactics and expenditures are making a difference.[3]

Three Arenas of Public Relations Practice

There are three broad arenas of public relations practice in which the public relations firm operates. These are sales support, public policy, and organizational effectiveness. Each of these arenas have specific functions (also known as functional areas), goals, clients, and collaborators that must be examined and taken into account when making a decision about the type of public relations that firm should be engaged (see Table 1.1).

Sales Support is the most traditional role of public relations. This is the area where public relations builds and maintains awareness for an organization's products or services while assisting marketing and sales in moving potential customers toward action. It also works with customer service and satisfaction issues. Many of the traditional media outreach activities of the field are part of sales support. Organizations often hire public relations firms for their media contacts, skill, and experience with events and awareness opportunities.

Public Policy is an arena of public relations that sometimes overlaps with public affairs, legal, or lobbying functions. The need in this area is ensuring that the Federal, State, and local rules and laws in place to do not hamper the ability of an organization to operate effectively and efficiently in the marketplace. Sometimes this means local zoning ordinances might be a problem, or State and Federal laws might get in the way. Taxes alone (those you have to pay as well as those that you may not want to pay) keep some public relations/public affairs functions very busy. Often corporate communication departments do not have the expertise or the connections to stay on top of potential issues or defeat or pass legislation that may arise or be needed. Demonstrating the organization is a positive

---

[3]See Bowen, Rawlins, and Martin (2010), pp. 24–35.

*Table 1.1[4] Three arenas of practice: How public relations serves &
adds value*

Sales Support	Public Policy	Organizational Effectiveness
Functions: Consumer relations Sell products & services Publicity & promotion Other marketing support Fundraising Enrollment, attendance at events Awareness Customer delight & Loyalty	*Functions:* Constituency relations Issues anticipation & tracking Crisis management Damage control Lobbying/government relations Community relations Social responsibility Contributions, focused philanthropy Volunteer programs	*Functions:* Employee & retiree relations Recruitment & retention Employee engagement Shareholder relations Financial relations Supplier relations Industry relations Alumni or member relations Change management
Goals: sales & profits, brand preference, market share, relationship marketing	*Goals:* maintain a hospitable environment & a cadre of active supporters	*Goals:* teamwork, one clear voice, motivation, productivity, loyalty, morale, understanding, cost-effectiveness, support
Clients: sales & marketing departments	*Clients:* CEO, Board, unit managers, senior managers	*Clients:* CEO, CFO, COO, unit managers
Collaborators: same as clients	*Collaborators:* law, strategic planning, risk management departments	*Collaborators:* human resources department, corporate secretary, quality or re-engineering teams, training units

and contributing member of the community is another part of this arena.
Public relations firms can assist with all these areas.

Finally, *Organization Effectiveness* is the third area where public relations
can make a difference—and a large one at that. Many of the issues that organizations have to deal with externally stem from *internal* communication
problems. Top down communications outlining what senior management
needs from employees and is trying to achieve is often not received, unheard,

---

[4]Patrick Jackson (1989, February 13). *pr reporter.*

or even acted upon. Bottlenecks can occur at all levels of the organization making communication difficult. Bottom up communication is also often blocked either because middle management does not want it going to the top, employees feel it will not matter if they do communicate upward, or senior managers do not or cannot hear what is being said as constructive. Finally, and often most difficult, is lateral communications—overcoming the "silo" mentality and departments that work at cross purposes, rather than as a team trying to achieve the same goals.

All of these are areas where organizations can suffer and public relations skills and techniques can help greatly. Before we move to describing how firms differ from each other, three points need to be emphasized:

1. **Public relations is a *staff*, not a line function.** Therefore, it is a **consulting & service position** which is always responsible to its **client.** Confusion arises when public relations tasks become a "product" (*e.g.,* a magazine in a membership organization or a user group to unite customers).

2. **Excellent public relations is about *outcomes*.** Any of the techniques or processes of public relations can be used in each of the arenas (*e.g.,* publications, events, publicity, speeches, one-on-one, symbolic communications), but the focus remains on what has been achieved on behalf of the organization's business goals (see Chapter 10 for a more complete discussion on outcomes).

3. **By nature public relations is *non-linear*, a seamless web.** Anything done in one arena affects the other arenas. Over-promising in sales support may bring a public policy response; lack of organizational effectiveness will affect sales, and so forth.

Sizes of Firms/Agencies

Having a handle on what types of work is needed when hiring a public relations firm can definitely help in narrowing the choices. There are public relations firms that are considered "large" in that they have multiple offices in many different cities and countries, each with a sizable staff of senior practitioners and junior associates. There also are mid-sized and small public relations firms.

Large Firms

One of the major benefits of large firms is their *reach*, both geographic and in terms of media and customer markets. Their breadth offers them the ability to have specialties in all areas of public relations (sales support, public policy, and organization effectiveness) and to work seamlessly across offices. Typically they have a research function that is skilled and integrated into support services for all their activities on the client's behalf. And they will most likely have had experience in your particular industry or situation regardless of what it is. Firms like this include Edelman (the largest in 2014), Weber Shandwick, Fleishman-Hillard , MSL Group, Burson-Marsteller, Hill & Knowlton, and Ketchum. Many of these firms have long and illustrious histories.

A drawback typically found with large firms or agencies is that the attention of senior managers is often focused on developing new business rather than servicing the client's account. So after the "sale" of getting their business, clients might see more junior account executives rather than the head honchos you met at the beginning. This can be an issue in other firms of all sizes, but large firms seem to be more prone to this shortcoming. Large firms are generally aware of this reputation and are sure to be careful to provide the appropriate top-level attention to the project. However, most likely there will be bigger clients with larger budgets on the docket who definitely have the potential to consume the firm's energy and time. Also, large firms are generally more expensive and the rates that are charged for more junior practitioners may be more than they are worth—skill wise. Patchy skills across offices is another drawback. But, depending on needs, a large firm with connections and reach may be just what a client wants.

Medium and Small Firms

Medium and small firms can offer a greater degree of attention from their senior members. Typically they have similar connections with the media in their *catchment area* (a geographical boundary that includes all readers of local/regional newspapers and viewers of broadcast/cable television) and, if they have specialties, they can have connections there as well. Some will have a wide range of expertise but it is usually more limited than the large firms. So, they may be highly skilled at sales support or public policy, but not organization effectiveness issues. Small firms are sometimes called "boutique" agencies or firms.

The medium to small firms have the flexibility to address a client's needs by often connecting with other small firms or independent professionals (see below) who can fill gaps in their capabilities. The benefit of this model is that you do not pay for what you do not need. There is no overhead cost to those functions that the client is not using. And the skills of the small firm professional can be wide and deep for they have had to do lots of different tasks and handled many different client types given their size. There is little ability to silo in a small firm. And, with a small firm clients may be the "large fish" and get the attention their business needs and deserves.

However, medium and small firms do not have the national or global reach that a large firm will have (although some are part of networks that can make those national & global connections such as GlobalCom, PRN, Global Network, and so forth.). And, if a lot of attention and work is needed, they may not have the depth of staff to cover your needs.

Independent professionals

Finally, there are *independent professionals*. These are professionals who often set themselves up as "So-and-So and Associates" to give the appearance of employing more than just one or two people. But these can also, depending on your needs, be your best bet. They can focus strictly on *your* needs and situation. They can function as an employee without the overhead and long-term costs of a full-time employee. They can give your public relations department flexibility and additional skills, creativity, fresh thinking and an extra pair of hands at a reasonable cost. Much like the smaller firms, the independent professional also offers boutique services, often in specialized areas that fit in with the area in which they practice.

Regardless of which direction a client might choose, it is important to first evaluate *your* needs. Firms of all sizes can offer senior managers a fresh perspective on the public relations function, what it can and should achieve, and the tools and tactics to get there. Evaluating your needs first will help make the search go much easier and you are more likely to find the right fit with less effort.

Each year a variety of publications that report on the profession publish a ranking of the top firms by a variety of indices including revenues and staff size. Many of these figures are self-reporting by the firms. Some publications do more detailed checking of the facts and figures submitted. These lists are by no means exhaustive and only include those firms that chose to participate or are legally allowed to reveal their numbers (for instance, those that are part of a larger holding company.) Figure 1.1 presents such a listing.

Public Relations/Advertising/Marketing

The next issue to address is the *focus* of the firm. For that reason, it is important to be aware of the difference between marketers, advertisers, and public relations firms.

In the field of communication, there are *marketing* professionals/agencies whose job it is to research and understand the motivations and behaviors of *customers* and *potential customers* so that they can craft products and services to meet their need (or create a need amongst them in order to sell a product or service). Marketers do not typically concern themselves with audiences other than customers or relationships beyond the sale.

Advertising professionals/agencies are typically paired with marketers because they too are typically *focused on producing ads for products and services* that the marketers have identified and researched. However, advertising agencies can also do advertising on reputational issues such as branding, social responsibility, community service, and shareholder/donor investment. That said, their work is primarily about creating *awareness* through one-way communication that is *paid* for by the client. And similar to marketing, advertising focuses on customers and relationships built around sales.

Public relations is responsible for *all* relationships with all publics and audiences an organization has—not just one segment. Any one of these publics can cause havoc for the organization so relationships need to be built and maintained constantly.

Rank 2014	Agency Name	2013 US Revenue ($)	2012 US Revenue ($)	Change %	Rank 2013	Staff 2013	Staff 2012	Change %	Revenue ($) per US employee	Location
1	Edelman	450,349,686	406,253,336	11%	1	2443	2249	9%	184,343	Chicago
2	Waggener Edstrom Communications	98,270,000	101,352,000	−3%	2	567	682	−17%	173,316	Bellevue, WA
3	APCO Worldwide	76,614,800	75,255,177	2%	3	295	288	2%	259,711	Washington, DC
4	W2O Group	69,680,000	56,097,000	24%	5	366	283	29%	190,383	San Francisco
5	FTI Consulting (1)	64,000,000	61,000,000	5%	4	205	220	−7%	312,195	New York
6	ICF SCM	48,135,325	42,826,374	12%	7	280	260	8%	171,912	Fairfax, VA
7	MWW	46,629,000	42,875,000	9%	6	210	207	1%	222,043	New York
8	ICR	43,322,436	37,339,790	16%	8	104	91	14%	416,562	Norwalk, CT
9	Finn Partners (2)	43,026,957	26,546,000	62%	11	287	205	40%	149,920	New York
10	Ruder Finn	37,444,000	33,704,000	11%	9	202	193	5%	185,366	New York

Figure 1.1 US Agency Rankings 2014 PR Week

Courtesy of *PR Week* (http://www.prweek.com/us/abr2014rankings)

There is a long-standing debate over what to call public relations. In the 1980s it went through the "Integrated Marketing Communications" phase. Prior to that professionals jumped from "Public Affairs" to "Public Information" to "Marketing Communications" and so on. Currently, "Strategic Communications" is a popular term for many. At the heart of the work done under all of these monikers is *building and maintaining mutually beneficial relationships*. That said, public relations is still a likely term you will find in a firm's name, even with all the negative connotations it carries (for instance, its [incorrect] association with "spin"). Therefore, when shopping for a firm, remember that you may encounter a variety of different titles which may or may not include the term "public relations."

Summary

To find the best "fit" when hiring a public relations firm, it is critical to understand the problems or opportunities your organization is facing and the type of expertise is necessary for solving those problems. The generalist firm can help identify issues by researching the situation and bringing past experience to the table. Likely, your issues will be related to one or more of the areas of "sales support," "public policy," or "organization effectiveness." Therefore, the firm you seek should have skills that align in one or more of these areas. Firms come in all sizes: large, medium, small (boutique), and independent professionals. Your situation analysis and scope of work will help the right size firm to interview. Understanding that public relations work is non-linear and outcomes focused will assist you in finding counsel who can guide you and your organization in building (or re-building) mutually supportive relationships with your audiences. Chapter 2 will further explore types of firms and their specialties.

CHAPTER 2

Types of Firms

We are a State university system that has unique issues with faculty, students and the all important alumni who are donors. We needed a firm that has experience dealing with the culture of academia. Building reputation requires a distinct understanding of the media hierarchy in higher education.

—Director of Communication, University System

Our issues were more about bridging differences with people, building awareness and relationships that mattered. We needed a firm that was expert in achieving these goals, not understanding the nuances and details of our business or industry. We could bring that to the table.

—VP of PR, Science and Technology Company

It certainly was an easier sell to my colleagues that the firm we brought in had previous experience with businesses like ours. But bottom line, once they were comfortable with the personalities involved and realized they were highly experienced people in the field, it didn't really matter.

—VP of PR, Health Care System

One of the most important questions someone seeking out a public relations firm will have to ask is this: *Do I want a firm that is an expert on my industry or an expert on my opportunity/problem?* If the answer is "both" then the pool of possible firms will likely narrow, but there are additional things to consider about your options.

There are firms who chose to develop *niche* or *boutique* practices to serve. The larger firms will have multiple niches. The medium or smaller firms may serve only one or a few. Often times it is because their leadership has spent time in that particular industry, knows it well, is comfortable with the challenges, structure, and opportunities that the industry presents.

From a marketing perspective, it is easier for a firm to network and be a presence in a particular industry line. The firm may become well-known and get recommendations from others in the industry with whom they work. The firms count on the fact that potential clients have respect for and interact with colleagues from the profession. And they may admire or want to emulate the institutions with who they are competitive. A question often asked of firms is, "With whom else in our industry have you worked?"

Industries That Firms Often Specialize In

There are many, many industries in which firms may specialize. The following is but a quick overview of typical industry specialization:

- Finance/banking/insurance
- Consumer product
- Industrial
- Travel/tourism/entertainment
- Utilities/energy
- Transportation
- Health care
- Education
- Social Services/not-for-profits
- Government
- Technology

Although the list is neither definitive nor exhaustive, these are some of the industries around which firms have built niches. Typically, when an industry booms, that specialty will be "marketed" by a firm. They often go out and find professionals who have worked in the industry to join them and market heavily to the industry from which they have been hired. APCO Worldwide, for instance, once a small-to-medium firm has become large—worldwide in presence—by bringing in professionals from a number of governmental sectors or industries.

Firms with specialized niches are more likely to have ongoing relationships with media contacts (both social and traditional) with foci in those specific areas. The benefit of this is that an organization may get faster, better coverage if it is media access and coverage you are seeking. However, if the firm has questionable or weak relationships with media contacts, then that may also rub off on the organization. It is important to be aware of the *tenor* and *tone* of the firm's relationships with their media contacts.

Finally, knowledge of—and experience with—a particular industry can definitely help reduce the learning curve of the firm and possible missteps that might occur if they are less familiar with the nuances, lingo, and culture of the trade. On the downside, the potential breadth and depth of "outside-the-box" thinking may be compromised by the limits of working within the same industry. Given human nature, the firm may succumb to the ease of doing the same old things, just for a different client. Organizations should make sure the team working with them has the professional training, development, and exposure that will allow them—no compel them—to seek new ideas that are specific and special to your situation.

Firms That Market by Specialty

Firms sometimes organize themselves to market by a particular area of practice rather than an industry. Much like the industry-based firms, it is often an area of practice that leadership either spends time doing in a previous position or profession and/or feels that their skills, knowledge, and interest support that niche. Some of the more common specialties include:[1]

- **Employee/Internal Communications:** This specialty deals with all types of internal communications including senior leadership counseling, training, coaching, messaging, speech

---

[1]For more on this, see: Harrison and Mühlberg (2014).

writing, research of communication systems, audits of communication flow, top-down messaging, feedback systems, improving lateral communications, Ambassador programs, and so forth. Some firms have integrated the fields of Organizational Behavior and Development into their practice and work on teaming issues, silo, and conflict management, and more.

- **Public Affairs:** Firms that specialize in public affairs typically have members who are experienced in government relations at the local, State, and/or Federal level. They specialize in keeping an organization's relationships with legislative representatives solid and their lines of communication open. They keep the representatives informed, track legislation that may impact your industry, and may lobby on your behalf.

- **Community Relations:** These firms work locally with communities where an organization is based or has offices/factories/warehouses. They are skilled in understanding individual communities and conducting outreach with "movers and shakers" (influential members of the community) who are important locally for your organization to operate without barriers. They often manage public service types of events, social responsibility programs, and so forth.

- **Media Relations:** Most common are firms that specialize in media relations. As social media grows, these firms are becoming even more prominent since the professionals who are "immigrants" to the social media onslaught look to the digital "natives" to help them find their way around the social media world. These firms are hyper-focused on the media, tracking who is where, writing about what, and influenced by whom in the social media realm and more. They know the mommy bloggers, the sports bloggers, the industry bloggers, the techie bloggers…. They are on top of Twitter, Facebook, Instagram, Tumbler, and the next social media phenomenon.

- **Financial/Investor Relations:** Firms that specialize in investor relations support the organization's need to build and retain relationships with investors and financial media. They may work on annual reports, quarterly statement announcements, counsel senior financial officers, write speeches, and participate in speakers' bureaus. Professionals in financial public relations firms typically will have a financial background from either working within the industry or through specialized education.

One of the benefits of retaining a firm with a particular specialty is that you get a high level of expertise in that particular arena. They know what they are doing; they have contacts and techniques that have been benchmarked and proven in all types of scenarios. They are experts in that particular field and will be current, if not at the forefront, of most new techniques and strategies.

The drawback, however, is that a specialty firm's hyper-focus makes them fairly narrow. If different needs arise outside their expertise, an organization will likely have to go and hire a different firm, starting a new relationship from scratch. And it will have to make sure the different firms all work together so that they speak with one clear voice to all organization stakeholders.

Allied Firms

There are many consultants and consulting firms whose core focus comes from fields other than public relations but believe that public relations is closely enough related to their body of knowledge and skill-base that they will attempt to serve as public relations counsel. It is important to understand their primary focus so as to be clear as to their proclivities when it comes to recommendations and advice.

A public relations professional/firm understands that their responsibility is to the organization *as a whole* and that any of the multitude of stakeholders can present serious problems if handled inappropriately. A public relations professional is always weighing how every decision, action, and word expressed by all parts of the organization will be interpreted by its stakeholders.

Fairly typical to this group are:

- **Marketing firms**—They are likely to seek businesses for branding, reputation management, customer outreach and service, and research. Their core focus is on the *customer* so they may lean toward a customer-centric approach in solving problems and seeking opportunities.
- **Human Resources**—Human resources are likely to seek *employee relations* projects including research, benchmarking, communications (particularly bottom up and lateral), and team building. Since employee relations is their core focus, they may see solutions as purely employee-based.
- **Law firms**—They sometimes try to handle public relations during crises, overseeing media response, stakeholder negotiations and relationships, union issues, or any stakeholder relationship related to a lawsuit for which they are responsible. Attorneys at times have been the most notorious for trying to control an organization's public relations, particularly its media responses, especially if the situation is tied to legal action.
- **Advertising agencies**—Similar to marketing firms, advertising agencies may be interested in assisting with branding issues, marketing campaigns, and customer outreach. With a traditional focus on *awareness building*, advertising agencies may lean toward a solution of media publicity (both social and traditional) for problem solving. However, many advertising agencies have created public relations arms that have a fuller, more robust view of the field and what it can and should do for a client. Organizations should always make sure they are dealing with an agency that has an independent public relations arm.

Naming and Titles

Finally, public relations firms tend to name their organizations anything *but* public relations. Their reticence to use the term "PR" in their firm name is based solely on the negative reputation that the field has experienced for decades as "spin doctors" and the many other negative connotations it brings up. Often public relations firms use other rather euphemistic language to position themselves in the marketplace and not be linked to public relations *per se*. These names vary widely from "Strategic Communications" (a newer nomenclature) to "Integrated Communication" to "Integrated Marketing Communication" to just plain "Communication." Many firms simply use the names of the partners and never mention public relations at all! Regardless of the name, it is important when you talk with them to understand their approach to the practice of public relations so as to gain the right fit with your organization.

Structures of Firms

Every firm has its own nuanced structure based on the leadership's preferences, operation culture, types of work done, and size. Senior professionals usually oversee junior associates, very similar to law firms.

In small firms, typically one partner/owner oversees business matters, and is likely responsible for management, client issues, and so forth. They most often work as a unified team on client projects with junior associates supporting whichever senior professional(s) and project(s) are engaged at the moment (see Figure 2.1). Small firms like these give younger associates a great variety of experience and exposure. Hierarchies and silos are usually not present in small firms, because everyone needs to pitch in to get the job done.

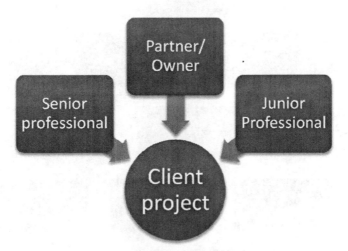

Figure 2.1 Small firm orientations to client project

A mid-size firm will often have a more robust staff with specific responsibilities. For instance, there is typically a designated business manager separate and apart from the professionals doing the work. There may be, in addition, financial managers, billing techs, support staff supervisors, and so forth. Junior associates may cluster around industries or specialties and be assigned to one or more senior professionals (partners) as a team to work on a particular client or sector. The junior associates may work on more than one client depending on the intensity of the work. There are often technical support groups in mid-size firms that work with all teams, for example, graphics, digital, and so forth.

Larger firms are mid-size firms on steroids. They have all the above and often are working not only across the country but across the world. Typically they will assign a team of junior professionals to a specific client and that is the only work that team does. The senior professionals may work on more than one client but junior associates do not. There are designated support groups for graphic development, digital development and management, research, and so forth.

Depending on the size of the firm, the structure might be hierarchal or flat—typically based on the organization's culture and preference of

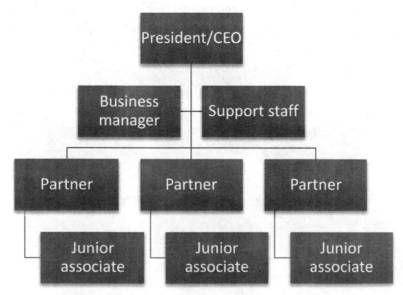

Figure 2.2 Typical mid-sized firm structure

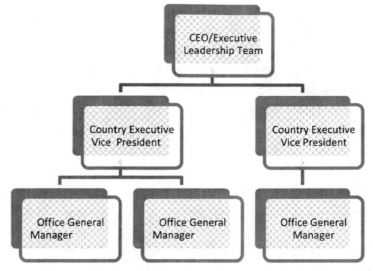

Figure 2.3 **A typical multinational public relations firm structure**

management. A large firm that has multiple offices in multiple countries will have a very complex structure, just like any multinational organization.

Within a particular office there is typically a head (be it the General Manager, President, CEO) with a variety of "Account Executives" or "Senior Counsel" reporting to the top. They may have teams reporting to them with titles like "Associate Counsel" or "Communication Specialist." These are usually less experienced professionals working as a team for a client. If the firm is slightly larger, they may have other "specialists" in media, technology, graphic design, or similar.

Summary

Firms typically market themselves in one of three ways—by *industry* (e.g., health care, higher education, technology), by *specialty* (e.g., internal communications, public affairs, community relations) or as *generalists*. Many firms blend specialties and industries, thus narrowing (or broadening) the arenas within which they work. Those who market by industry typically have an in-depth understanding of that area and likely hire employees who have worked in that industry. Those who market by specialty will likely have experience across many industries in that particular specialty arena. Generalists typically have worked in a wide variety of industries and specialties and bring a more versatile skill base to address any and all relationship problems that might arise. Allied firms (marketing, advertising, legal) occasionally dip into the public relations business but their sightlines can skew them from seeing the big picture. Finally, what public relations firms call themselves can vary significantly. It is important to remember that whatever the firm is called, the profession is about building relationships that support and protect your organization's bottom line. Chapter 3 will take you through the steps for hiring the right firm.

CHAPTER 3

Hiring a Firm

Our internal Public Relations leadership understood the breadth of the problems we were facing and the skill base and expertise that was needed from an external firm. They made a recommendation and after one meeting we started work together.

—ED of NPO

If the project is well-defined and specific to a particular project, we typically put out an RFP. But it takes a fair amount of time to put that together and then review all the responses before interviewing can even begin.

—Public Affairs Manager, Government Entity

We have a firm with whom we have an ongoing relationship. Typically we start with them. If it is a situation or project that they do not specialize in, they recommend others with whom we can talk. I trust their judgment since they know us and our needs.

—VP, Communications, Health Care Organization

I am constantly being called by firms seeking to 'have lunch' or a meeting to 'get to know them.' Honestly, I am way too busy for that! If and when we have a need, I call my colleagues in other organizations and ask them who they use, who they recommend. I go almost totally by word-of-mouth.

—Senior VP, Public Relations, Technology Firm

I attend a lot of conferences where I hear speakers on a variety of topics. Sometimes I will hear someone who makes an impression. I may reach out to them if I have a situation that requires their type of expertise—once I've checked with colleagues on their reputation, etc.

—Director of Communications, Higher Education Institution

We favor firms who are involved in their profession through their professional societies, those that value ongoing professional development, giving back and sharing knowledge. We feel that if they value those types of activities, they likely are broad thinkers who have greater exposure than just serving clients. Also, professional credentials carry a great deal of weight in our book—APR and such.

—VP, PR, Airline Industry

There are a variety of methodologies for finding the right firm for any particular situation. However, before you start making calls, it is important to understand the problem at hand so as to hire a firm with the right skills and direct them at the right problems/opportunities. When determining who to invite to the table to even *discuss* an opportunity, it is very important to be clear about what the organization is seeking—even if it is the need for help in figuring out what is going on. In Chapter 2, we discussed the type of firms you might want to interview about your situation—industry based, specialty based, and allied. The analysis of the issues being faced by the organization will help guide these decisions ultimately.

With this information in hand, as the communications professional you now need to find with whom you want to discuss your situation. Using "word-of-mouth" is the best resource at this point. Look around for organizations that may have experienced what you are facing in the past. Who did they use for public relations counsel? Do not get stuck looking only at organizations in your industry because most public relations situations cross industry borders. Try asking yourself the following questions:

- Are we being hounded by local media? Who else in town has been the target of local media angst?
- Are we facing internal stakeholder communication issues? Who do you know from our business or social connections that have also had internal issues?
- Is there a potential legal issue? Ask your external legal counsel whom they know and have worked with in the past.
- Do we need to build awareness or do branding for the organization? What organization has effective graphics and the reputation that you would love to also have?

- Is there a speaker or author on the subject of public relations who has acknowledged expertise in the area of need?
- Who in the business community serves on a Board of a local nonprofit or service organization on which you serve knows public relations? Who do they know? Hire?

The only danger in word-of-mouth referrals is when someone has a "friend" or "brother-in-law" who does "Public Relations." Without some personal experience with their work or performance, this is a risky chance to take. However, with some careful screening you can be more assured of the work and professionalism of those you choose to interview.

There are a number of elements to consider when looking for a public relations firm. Some elements to consider in this screening phase include:

- *Are they members of a professional Public Relations organization* (e.g., Public Relations Society of America (PRSA), International Association of Business Communicators(IABC), International Public Relations Society of America (IPRSA), National School Public Relations Association (NSPRA), Canadian Public Relations Association (CPRS)?
- *Are they credentialed by that organization in any way?* For example, PRSA members have their Accreditation in Public Relations (APR), while IABC members have their Accredited Business Communicator (ABC).
- *Do they serve on any Boards, nonprofit or otherwise?*
- *Do they have an educational background in the field, either undergraduate or graduate?*

It is important to see that the firm's leadership takes their understanding and practice of the profession seriously, that they adhere to a Code of Ethics (Bowen et al. 2010; Harrison and Mühlberg 2014), and that they are constantly seeking to advance their own knowledge if not that of their profession—just as others who are in your line of work. Without some sort of screening, you may end up with a firm with serious ethical issues that can backfire on your own organization—something you do not want to have to deal with at all.

Request for Proposal or Face-to-Face Meetings?

Now it is time to decide whether to put your organization's public relations needs out there as a *Request for Proposal* (RFP) or just invite those firms on your narrowed down list for a "meet and greet" get-together (Stacks 2011; Michaelson and Stacks 2014).

Requests for Proposals

Requests for Proposals are fairly sterile documents that outline the scope of work that the organization believes it requires: parameters for the work, timelines, and other sundry elements that might be required by the accounting department, ethical/legal standards, human resources requirements, and various other requirements. The RFP does not give the competing firms much leeway in how they might go about solving the organizations problems or meeting its opportunities. Often times, it comes down to a "price"—and firms know this.

The main complaints about RFPs from a firm's perspective are fourfold:

1. The time they take to complete;
2. The scope of work is vague (not wanting to air the organization's issues);
3. They are often poorly written; and
4. The "shot in the dark" aspect (the firm must spend time putting together ideas for an organization with whom they do not have a relationship).

RFPs set up the quintessential vendor–client relationship, which does not preclude getting good counsel but does not promote it either.

If your organization chooses—or is required—to use the RFP process, make sure the following elements are included:

- *Reason for RFP*—Why now, what is going on in the organization and/or industry?
- *Background*—What is the history or reason for the project?

- *Scope of Work*—What are the specific requirements concerning objectives, how outcomes will be measured (versus outputs), timelines, budget range, and any restrictions?
- *What or who are the points of contact*—with phone numbers and email addresses?
- *What is the timeline for RFP process*—including when questions from responding firms will be accepted, when responses to those questions can be expected in return, whether conference calls will be allowed, decision deadlines, and so forth?
- *What are the requirements for professional services*, such as adherence to Codes of Ethics, insurance requirements, languages?
- *What are the organization's preferences*, if any (e.g., women/minority owned, industry experience, specialty experience, and so on)
- *Is there a requirement for bios* for the entire work team?
- *Will the project end in a case study* (if desired)?

Once the RFPs are submitted and screened, it is still critically important to bring in the finalist(s) to make sure the fit with the organization is good. Sometimes those on paper just do not make the cut face-to-face.

And finally, if going the RFP route, you can send it to the firms that have been identified as perhaps being a good fit for your organization. The firms identified may or may not respond to the RFP—given some of the drawbacks of doing so—so research may have to begin anew with the firms that do respond.

Face-to-Face Introductory Meeting

If the work involved in managing an RFP is not exciting and your organization is not required to put one out, then a simple meeting is another (and perhaps better) alternative. Invite the two or three firms identified earlier as possible counsel at different times to discuss the scope of your organization's needs and what they may bring to the table to help you achieve your objectives.

This discussion can flow in many ways. Some firms like to do a formal ("dog and pony") presentation about their skills, experience, and attributes. Others would rather have an informal conversation about your organization's issues, needs, and their experience meeting those needs. Expectations need to be set ahead of time and each firm should know them. Leave plenty of time between meetings (different days) rather than marching them in every 2 hours on the same day; such a plan reduces your stress and fatigue.

What to Cover

There are a number of important things that need to be discussed when talking to potential public relations firms. Minimally, the following are essential to better understand the organization's needs and the firm's ability to meet your needs:

- What is the *situation your organization is facing* and why? What do you believe you need a firm to come in and do (the "Scope of Work")?
- What is the *firm's experience in this area*? For what similar projects and clients have they done this type of work? What was their experience and what type of outcomes did they obtain?
- What would be their *general approach*? Why? What theoretical or strategic basis is there for their approach? How would they measure success?
- Who *would be involved* on the team and who would be your *main contact* on the project?
- What are their *billing rates*? Do they differ for various levels of talent, work product, other? (For more on billing, see Chapter 5.)
- *References* (if the word-of-mouth recommendations need further exploration)?

If the fit seems good, ask them to put together a *Scope of Work* that includes their approach, objectives, deliverables, projected outcomes and a way to measure them, a timeline, and budget. Compare this against the other firms' Scope of Work if you have more than one firm bidding on your work. (Scope of Work is covered in detail in Chapter 4).

This document, along with reference checks and your gut feeling from the meetings, will indicate if the firm "gets" what it is you want from them. The budget is usually negotiable, so push back if you want to work with them but the numbers are too high for the organization's budget. A good firm will work to meet your needs without busting your bottom line!

Ongoing Counsel

Employing an in-depth interview methodology (Michaelson and Stacks 2014; Stacks 2011) is also useful if the organization is seeking a firm to be your "ongoing counsel."[1] Having a firm available that stays on top of your organization's and industry's issues can be very useful in three important ways:

1. *When things get sticky.* You can handle it, but need an objective third party who knows your organization and industry to provide a "sanity check." For instance, you are working on a sensitive document that needs a look from someone with understanding of stakeholders and their reaction, a CEO speech, and so forth.
2. *Third-party credibility.* Occasionally, after a period of time in an organization it can become more difficult to be a "prophet in your own backyard." It can be useful to be able to say that you have talked with "outside counsel" and they recommended or confirmed a particular approach. Or you can even bring them to the management table to

---

[1]When firms use the term "counsel" they are indicating that they actively engage with the client in all matters that might impact on the client's needs, to include meeting with the company's Board of Directors, Chief Executive Officer, Human Relations officer, Chief Communication Officer, and others. In other words, they take an active role in the decision-making process. An excellent discussion of this can be found in John W. Hill's 1963 book, *Becoming a Public Relations Man.*

make what has to be said stronger or gain some distance for something that may be distasteful.

3. *Internal staffing/workload decisions.* If your departme\nt needs some objective analysis (skills, responsibilities, organization) a firm can provide objective feedback if they have any organizational development (OD) experience. Or, when things get too busy, you can kick some of the excess work to them; there is no need to bring a new group up to speed.

It is important to establish how the ongoing counsel relationship will be billed prior to making a decision. We discuss the various billing methods used by firms in Chapter 5. Your budget and their rates may influence your final decision.

Summary

The process of finding the right public relations firm starts with the decision to go either with an RFP or with personal meetings. The RFP route suggests that you are absolutely sure of the problem/opportunity to be addressed and the actions that need to be taken. It requires a firm to put together a strict plan of action and budget to meet your needs. It does not allow much room for miscalculation as to the problem or the solution. The personal meeting approach allows for a free-flow conversation and the opportunity to sense if the firm "gets" your needs and problems. Finding firms for either method requires some research. Ask organizations and colleagues who have faced similar situations for their recommendations. Go to professional organizations for lists of local, regional, and national firms that might address your needs. Take note of firms whose members are credentialed (i.e., APR, ABC), and who value professional development for their staff along with staff having educational backgrounds in communication (not just journalism). Finally, firms that ascribe to a Code of Ethics are the best partners. Chapter 4 will help you define the work that is to be done by your newly hired firm.

CHAPTER 4

Defining the Work

We were knee deep in a project with a firm when we realized they were on a different track from us. They were pursuing goals that we had not agreed to!

—Executive Director, Nonprofit Organization

Our experience was great because we had clearly identified what the problems were and had carefully identified what we needed done.

—CEO, Mid-Size Manufacturer

We thought we knew what we needed until Phase 1 of the work had been done and the research showed we were off target completely with what we thought was going on. The firm we had hired though re-worked the Scope of Work and we got back on track quickly.

—VP, PR, Health Care

It is difficult sometimes, until we are fully immersed in the client work to lay out a clear path start to finish. We lay out our work and come to an agreement on everything we can see ahead of time but try to work phase by phase staying in constant contact with the client if anything needs to change.

—Partner, Mid-Size PR Firm

A successful working partnership with a firm comes most easily by clearly defining expectations at the beginning. That arises from a good working *relationship*, open and regular communication, and a clear *Scope of Work* outlining the project in its entirety if possible or as much as can be defined to start.

A Scope of Work (see Figure 4.1) is the contract between a public relations firm and an organization defining what the situation is at the present moment, what the firm will be doing to assist the organization, what they will be delivering in terms of products and services, and how success will be measured. It should be established up front and revisited along the way to make sure the direction and implementation is going as anticipated. Not every Scope of Work is the same. Different projects require different pieces to be included. The following are "typical" for a good Scope of Work.

Scope of Work Contents

The Scope of Work is a document that outlines to what degree the firm is knowledgeable about the problem or opportunity, has the capability to offer solutions to that problem or take advantage of the opportunity, and has the experience and staff to actually complete the mission if the organization hires it. All Scope of Work documents begin with an understanding of the situation.

An Understanding of the Situation

A clearly written "understanding" section shows that the firm has a clear grasp of what is going on from the organization's perspective, what may have gotten it to this point, and what its needs are at the start. This may change along the way, however. The firm will do an analysis on what *the organization* feels is the problem or opportunity and may find that the root issue or need is different than what you first assumed. At that point a revised or updated "understanding" should be developed, for this likely will also change other aspects of the Scope of Work.

Situation Understanding Example (also see Figure 4.1 above)

Organization XYZ wants to raise the visibility of XYZ's quality, services, and locations among target audiences. In addition to attracting new clients, XYZ would like to help members keep their current clients as competition increases.

Scope of Work
For: In-Trouble Technology

Situation Understanding
(This section outlines the situation as it is understood by the firm.)
Client is a small, private technology firm with a base of 100 employees who work both at the main location and on the road servicing customers' needs. It has been in business since 1998 and has had a good reputation with customers and within the local community. Its employees and management are active in the community, serve on community nonprofit boards, and hold local government elected positions. Recently, questions have been raised that employees in elected positions have been directing contracts away from their competitors and to their own business. Though this isn't true and there is no evidence of this activity, the rumor mill is continuing to feed this story.

Our Approach
(This section summarizes the strategy or approach the firm seeks to employ to help with the problem or opportunity.)
Rumors, unfortunately, tend to take on a life of their own if not dealt with in a timely and thorough fashion. And they have a habit of popping up again from time to time. It is important to deal with the rumor and replace it in the minds of those who have heard it with alternative, positive connections. Research and case studies on rumor management show that a series of steps must be taken to put the rumor down including third-party support, checks and balances, and blanketing strategies. FIRM will adopt use of all these strategies and more.

Goals & Objectives
(This section lays out the goals and objectives of the project with some detail.)
Goal: To stop transmission of this rumor completely within the community and replace and re-enforce with a positive understanding, thus enhancing reputation.
Objective 1: Understand the depth and breadth of the rumor so as to target appropriate action without spreading the rumor further (80 percent within two weeks).
Objective 2: Establish systems and strategies within organization and related institutions for assuring positive reputation (100 percent within one month).
Objective 3: Build and implement blanketing strategies to remove negative cognition and re-enforce and/or establish positive cognition with the organization (25 percent within 6 weeks, 50 percent within 12 weeks, 75 percent within 18, and 100 percent within 24 weeks).

Phases of Work
(This section lays out the work in some detail, often by phases, with estimated budgets if possible.)
Phase 1: Conduct research with key audiences to gain insight into awareness and knowledge levels.
Estimated timeline: 3 weeks
Estimated cost of professional services: $xxxx.xx
Phase 2: On the basis of an understanding from the research, design strategy along with any necessary materials (talking points, ethics codes, and so on) necessary for implementation of strategy.
Estimated timeline: 2 weeks
Estimated cost of professional services: $xxxx.xx
Phase 3: Implement strategy as detailed in Phase 2; ongoing counsel with client
Estimated timeline: 24 weeks
Estimated cost of professional services: $xxxx.xx
Phase 4: Evaluation and follow-up based on initial research; includes dipstick research as part of implementation of strategy.
Estimated timeline: 2 weeks
Estimated cost of professional services: $xxxx.xx
Total estimated budget range for Phases I – IV: $xxxxx.xx
Out-of-pocket expenses estimate: $xxxx.xx

Figure 4.1 An example of scope of work

There are misperceptions that once individuals get insurance, they need to leave the XYZ to make room for other customers . . . XYZ wants to communicate that they can, and want to, serve everyone.

The XYZ wants to conduct internal research to understand not only perceptions and communication preferences internally, but also likely behaviors of staff around recommending and promoting XYZ services to current client family and friends.

XYZ has requested this firm to assist the communications committees with the incorporation of all the ideas and settle on a course of action that could realistically be undertaken by all those involved.

Approach

This section typically lays out the strategy the firm will follow to address the situation and why. It may discuss theoretical underpinnings for its approach, strategic decisions, and a rationale for the direction recommended to be taken on behalf of your organization. It may cite case examples, statistics, or other data to support its approach. It may also lay out the nuances or caveats that the approach may encounter that could alter or change the strategy going forward. The approach section should give a clear sense of their direction and goals for the project or campaign.

Approach Example (also see Figure 4.1 above)

Research and experience shows that word-of-mouth is the most optimum strategy for stimulating behavior. The Public Relations Behavioral Model (Jackson 1990a, 1990b, 1996) shows that once Awareness is attained and Latent Readiness is built, social connections linked with Triggering Events are most effective in moving behavior. The strategy to obtain the goals sought by XYZ corporation will use this model to guide ABC firm in meeting the needs of XYZ corporation.

In order to raise awareness levels, in Phase One we will conduct research to ascertain current levels of awareness and reaction to messaging and messengers. In Phase Two we will seek to build latent readiness through a series of one-way and two-way communication vehicles along with peer connections. In Phase Three we will launch a number of Triggering Events that will stimulate behaviors among Innovators and Early Adopters to gauge readiness of quick-to-act stakeholders. This will give a sense of the effectiveness of work to date and how to tweak activities and vehicles to stimulate Early and Late Majority toward behavior. These early measures will be replicated with later Trigger Events aimed at additional publics. Finally we will evaluate outtakes as part of the tweaking activities with dipsticks of reaction and observation of behaviors. Outcomes will be evaluated with formal research tools.[1]

Goals and Objectives

Next, the Scope of work should identify the goals that the firm will seek to achieve. Goals are general statements of what needs to be accomplished (Michaelson and Stacks 2014; Stacks and Bowen 2013, p. 13). Objectives should be specific and measureable (Stacks 2011). Objectives are typically listed by stakeholder group and should point the way toward particular levels of awareness/information, motivation and behavior. Both should support the goals of the organization's business plan.

Example (see also Figure 4.1 above)

Goal 1: Build employee ambassador program to assist with organizational reputation building.

Objectives:

- Increase awareness and understanding of employees as to the importance and impact of the ambassador program by 60 percent in year one.
- Increase employee behavior through participation in "foot-in-door" activities by 20 percent in year one.

---

[1]See Chapter 10 for a more in-depth discussion of outtakes and outcomes.

- Increase employee commitment to long-term ambassador commitments by 10 percent in year one.

Goal 2: Increase client attachment and connection to organization .

Objectives:

- Increase client awareness and understanding of the advantages of organizational services and activities by 30 percent within 6 months.
- Increase client positive motivation toward organizational services and activities by 20 percent within 6 months.
- Increase recommendations by clients of organizational services and activities to friends and family by 10 percent within 6 months (and an additional 5 percent within 1 year).

Methodology

This section is included if the work requires research as a precursor to the actual activities. It describes what type of research with what target audience and sampling details.

Phases of Work

The work is often clustered into *phases*. It systematically organizes the work for both the organization and the firm. It can also be a tool for budgeting and budget negotiations. If the budget is too high, it is easier to see where things might be trimmed by bringing portions in-house or by rethinking strategy or tools. It also offers points at which to stop and check that the next phase is in fact appropriate and necessary given what is done and learned in earlier phases.

Deliverables

Deliverables are what you can expect in terms of work product and are also known as *output*.[2] They should be laid out by the appropriate phase

---

[2]See Chapter 10 for a complete discussion on outputs.

if possible. These sometimes change as more is learned about stake-holders and their needs and motivation, but can be modified along the way.

Evaluation

Here the firm should explain how they will measure what it is they are doing and how success is defined in terms of output, outtakes, and out-comes (see Chapter 10 for a full discussion on Evaluation.) Measurement should relate directly to the goals and objectives that have been estab-lished for the project (Michaelson and Stacks 2011, 2014).

Timeline and Budget

The timeline and budget are often laid out by each phase of the project. Firms sometimes prefer to estimate the timeline by number of weeks or months rather than specific dates. This is because they cannot control what goes on within your organization that might delay decisions or pre-dict intervening events. So always assume the timeline will not reflect a perfect world and make sure you build in time for glitches, slowdowns, holidays, and other events that may interrupt the project. Most timelines

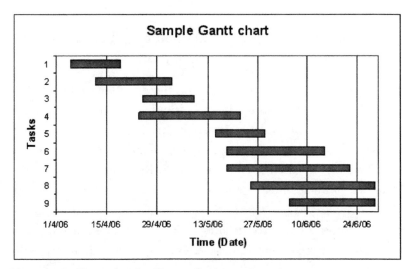

Figure 4.2 Example of a Gantt chart

are presented in the form of a Gantt chart (see Figure 4.2) where each goal and its objectives are plotted over time from beginning to end of the project with specific benchmarks often included to determine if the particular phase is on schedule—this is often called being "on phase and on schedule" in updating reports.

The obvious exception to this is if the project has a "drop dead" date— an event that has a date certain (election, shareholder meeting, product introduction, and so forth). In this situation, the timeline should work backward from the "drop dead" or final due date.

The Scope should not only identify estimated billable professional time but also estimate expenses. (You can read more about how budgets are laid out and billing is done in Chapter 5.)

Team Members

The Scope of Work will typically identify who is lead counsel for the project, their background, experience, and typically their billing rates. Depending on the size of the firm and their structure, they may also list other team members along with the experience, biography, and billable rate on this project. This section of the Scope protects your understanding that the professionals you have met with will be doing the work to which you have agreed.

Memorandum of Understanding/Letters of Agreement

The Scope of Work is your contract with the firm about the project itself and how it will be carried out. In addition to this document you may also have a *Letter of Agreement* (see Figure 4.3) or a *Memorandum of Understanding* that lays out the working relationship and issues around confidentiality, Intellectual Property Rights, Reproduction and Use of Materials, insurance needs, compensation details, termination clauses, Hold Harmless statements, and a myriad of other legal requirements that your organization's attorneys require or, if you are government-funded, are required by regulation. A non-disclosure agreement is also typically included to cover confidentiality issues.

Date

This letter of agreement defines the scope and terms for services to be performed for IN-TROUBLE TECHNOLOGY by PUBLIC RELATIONS FIRM.

Scope of Services

FIRM will provide consulting services as spelled out in the Scope of Work. This will include:

1) SUMMARY
2) SUMMARY
3) SUMMARY

Deliverables

- DETAIL
- DETAIL
- DETAIL

Budget

- Professional Services will be billed (HOW AND BY WHEN) a total "not to exceed" amount without discussion and/or contract changes
- FIRM will bill at the rate of $XXX an hour for senior counsel, $XXX an hour for associate counsel, $XX an hour for paraprofessionals, and $XX an hour for administrative support. Time spent on the project will be tracked (HOW?).
- Out-of-pocket expenses (for postage, telephone, deliveries, travel, vendors, materials, and so on) will be billed at cost, without markup.

Terms and Conditions

Billing and Payment

FIRM will invoice SCHEDULE.

Payment is requested within XX days of receipt of invoice. Invoices that remain outstanding for payment for more than XX days may result in suspension of work, (OTHER)

Ownership of Products

FIRM agrees to protect the confidentiality and integrity of proprietary information gathered, ongoing counsel and materials produced, and will not share any information publicly without the client's consent. Work done under this Agreement will be "work for hire." However, FIRM retains the right to use work created under this Agreement for marketing of services by FIRM.

This letter will serve as the formal contract between FIRM and CLIENT. If it is consistent with your understanding, please sign both copies and return one to FIRM.

Figure 4.3 Sample letter of agreement

Summary

The document describing the parameters of the work your firm will be doing for you is often called a "Scope of Work." It typically outlines the firm's understanding of the situation, their approach to the project/situation, goals and objectives, and specific activities, often broken down into "Phases" of work. Deliverables are also laid out along with how the firm will measure what they are doing on your behalf in terms of outputs, outtakes, and outcomes.[3] A timeline (sometimes in Gantt form) and budget (see Chapter 5) will also be included. Lead counsel will typically be identified with biographic information along with names and biographies of those who will function on their team. Billing rates are sometimes included. The Scope of Work becomes the basis for your contract with the firm (Memorandum of Understanding or Letter of Agreement) and should be re-visited often to make sure everything is on target or else modified based on new information or events. Typically some communication will occur related to the changes in the project plan and the budget. It may be informal (just a written communication that acknowledges the changes and budget increase). If it is a major change then the Scope of Work is modified with budget and re-issued. The Letter of Agreement or MOU typically is not changed. Chapter 5 will discuss in more detail how firms bill.

---

[3]For definitions of terms, see Stacks and Bowen (2013).

CHAPTER 5

How Firms Bill

My budget is very tight and I must know my external counsel costs up front to the penny.

—Executive Director, Non-Profit Organization

We were in the middle of a crisis—we arrived at an "upset" number together at which the firm would let us know when we hit—but we knew it was going to take some unexpected budget to resolve.

—VP, PR, Fortune 500 Company

We use a variety of billing models depending on the needs of the client. They are all doable.

—Partner, Mid-Size Consulting Firm

There are eight basic billing models typically used by public relations firms; hourly rate, blended rate, retainer, value, project, package, performance, and full time equivalent (FTE) model. This chapter will explain each and discuss the various pros and cons associated with the model from the perspective of the client and the public relations firm. Understanding these billing models will help you, your procurement expert, and the organization better understand the tangible and financial business values presented by your public relations firm. Hopefully, this knowledge also leads to smooth and successful negotiations with your firm.

Billing Models[1]

Hourly Rate Model

The *hourly rate model* is pretty straightforward. Each hour of firm activity is billed according to a schedule established by the firm. Firms usually require their employees to log each hour of work in 15-minute increments. The employee usually enters a work code, which translates into the type of work and client being served and will often include brief comments. This information is typically used later to form the basis of the firm's periodic report to the client (see Chapter 7). Similar to law, accounting, and other professional service firms, hourly rates are tied to the level of experience

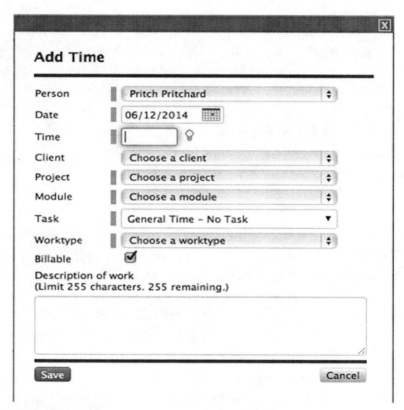

Figure 5.1 Project management software example used to track the time spent on projects

[1] Boehler, S., Smith, T. A., and Stier, K. (2005). "Professional Services Industry Billing Practices." Mercer Island Group, LLC. Retrieved from http://findpdf.net/reader/Professional-Service-Industry-Billing-Practices-Mercer-Island-Group.html.

that is brought to bear on the activity. Senior professionals will bill at a higher rate than more junior, entry-level practitioners.

One of the benefits of the hourly rate model is that it provides more transparency in billings. It is also a billing method that is easily tracked for both the firm and the client. Public relations firms are able to provide adequate staffing, which usually results in value tied directly to pre-agreed objectives. Payment is for work done on a real-time/real-use basis and is typically the best billing method for clients requesting specific staff members on a particular project. Out-of-pocket expenses (e.g., printing costs, binders, postage, and mileage) are billed separately. Most firms bill for the actual out-of-pocket expense, but some add a 10 percent to 15 percent markup. The hourly rate model is often preferred by procurement experts.

One downside of the hourly rate model is the potential for the client to feel as if they are being nickel-and-dimed. Critics also object to having to pay more for "slow" people. The hourly rate model also creates pressure to take senior people off the account or project, because they cost more than junior people. This, in turn, tends to force the work to the most junior, and inexperienced, level.

Another potential downside to the hourly rate model is "clock watching." The firm necessarily needs to account for its billable hours so as not to exceed the contract. If the contracted-for hours are exceeded, the firm either has to "eat" the extra time, go back to the client for more money, or stop work altogether. It also encourages firms to bill for *execution* instead of *strategy*. It is often difficult for a client to place value in thinking.

From the client side, "watching the clock" cannot only add stress, but also potentially inhibit results. Focusing on how much a meeting with the entire account team is costing takes the focus off solving the problem, meeting the challenge, or seizing the initiative. Clients also tend to focus on execution and miss the strategy under the hourly billing model.

Blended Rate Model

The *blended rate model* is similar to the hourly rate model except that one hourly rate is used for *all* firm employees assigned to the account. Out-of-pocket expenses are billed at cost or with the standard firm markup. This model works well for big teams involving many different team members of different levels of expertise and experience. It also helps balance out situations where work is split between senior and junior staff. Advocates of this model opine that it provides blended and fair economics to clients.[2] Critics say this model does not provide for the ebb and flow of a client's business.[3]

> The blended rate model helps balance costs when both junior and senior staff work on a project together.

Retainer or "Fixed Fee" Model

Many in the public relations industry prefers the *retainer model* of billing. Sometimes called "fixed fee," the client pays a set amount either monthly or annually under this model. Out-of-pocket expenses are billed at cost or with the standard firm markup. Proponents of this model emphasize that the focus is on *outputs*,[4] not the amount of time spent working on the project. Similarly, others say the retainer arrangement puts the emphasis on producing results regardless of the time needed to produce those results and makes the firm accountable for getting the job done. Retainers help clients avoid the ebb and flow of public relations activities and make invoicing easier for the clients. This is especially attractive if the client is removed from the procurement or accounts payable department, removing the requirement to explain why one month is more or less than another. It also eliminates surprises and contentious billing problems. From the firm's perspective, this model provides for steady

---

[2] Croft, A.C. (2006). *Managing a Public Relations Firm for Growth and Profit*, 2nd ed. Binghampton, NY: Hayworth Press. p. 200.

[3] Boehler et al., p. 13.

[4] An output is defined by Stacks and Bowen (2013, 21) as "What is generated as a result of a PR program or campaign that may be received and processed by members of a target audience, and may have cognitive impact on outtakes: the way a target audience or public feels, thinks, knows, or believes; the final stage of a communication product, production, or process resulting in the production and dissemination of a communication product (brochure, media release, website, speech, and so on). . . the number of communication products or services resulting from a communication production process; the number distributed and/or the number reaching a targeted audience; sometimes used as an outcome serving as a dependent variable in research." Chapter 10 contains a more complete discussion of this concept.

and dependable income. It also encourages efficiency and high performance on the firm's side. The downside, though, is it is easy for scope creep to occur so the firm ends up spending more hours than it thought when the retainer was first calculated.

Critics of the retainer model worry that both sides of the relationship could become comfortable and therefore lazy in managing processes and the overall work.[5] Others complain that retainers are inflexible by nature and do not reflect the vagaries of public relations work. Some are concerned about the lack of accountability inherent in the retainer model. Firms are concerned about the client taking unfair advantage of the retainer relationship by demanding more effort than has been budgeted, thus impacting the firm's profitability.

Value Model

The *value model* is a billing method that relies on the value of the benefit provided to the client and not the mechanics of the process. It is a highly sought after billing method for public relations. Here the firm utilizes a results-driven pricing strategy charging a predetermined and agreed fee based on *mutually* determined goals and objectives.

The obvious benefit of this billing model is the client pays for *quantifiable results*, a focus on *outcomes* instead of outputs.[6] Clients are guaranteed their goals will be met. This billing model is favored by firms and clients alike, because it fosters a strong relationship between the two parties. Proponents point out that the value model eliminates the conflicts of interest built into the hourly billing system.

On the downside, it remains difficult for public relations to prove its value (see Michaelson and Stacks 2014, pp. 3–76). Procurement experts especially indicate difficulty with this billing model. The primary challenge is defining *success*; what quantitative and qualitative metrics and experiences will

---

[5]Boehler et al., p. 13.

[6]An outcome is defined by Stacks and Bowen (2013, 21) as "Quantifiable changes in awareness, knowledge, attitude, opinion, and behavior levels that occur as a result of a public relations program or campaign; an effect, consequence, or impact of a set or program of communication activities or products, and may be either short term (immediate) or long term."

be used and how will they be measured. Obviously, sales growth is an outstanding and commonly used quantitative success metric. But it is difficult to know how much of that sales growth is attributable to the public relations effort. Firms avoid business growth as a measurement of success because they have limited control over the dynamics of that growth or the business environment. Increased awareness and changes in attitudes are difficult success metrics to use without a significant investment in research and evaluation (see Michaelson and Stacks 2014), something for which many clients are not willing to pay. Similarly, behavior change is difficult to measure and evaluate.

Project Billing Model

Project billing involves a set fee for a definable activity such as a branding effort, complete corporate identity package, direct mail campaign, trade show event, or business or marketing plan. Public relations firms either have set rates for these projects or estimate the length of time to complete and provide a project cost to the client. The client is billed the project cost whether it takes more or fewer hours to complete. With project billing, the client does not receive a cost breakdown of the hours spent on the project.

This billing model is most beneficial when the tactical aspects of the project tend to be expensive or involve high out-of-pocket cost activities. Public relations firms argue that project billing gives the firm the ability to bill for specific tactics or projects that come up, but are not covered in the Scope of Work, especially when the client is on retainer.[7] The project billing model is generally *not* good for building long-term relationships. Some firms using the project model provide an estimate only, subsequently billing for actual time incurred. This has obvious drawbacks and potential clients should evaluate the experience and special expertise of the firm carefully to determine how close the estimate is likely to be to actual cost.

Package Model

Closely resembling the project model is the *package model* of billing. The public relations firm charges for packaged or prestructured services such

---

[7] Boehler et al., p. 14.

as a branding workshop, media training session, strategic planning sessions, executive off-sites, and the like. Package models offer the client very specific services with specific deliverables from the public relations firm. These services are often above and beyond those considered part of a retainer arrangement. The major advantage of the package model is that the public relations firm knows precisely the scope of effort and the client knows exactly what they are getting in return.

Performance-Based Compensation Model

Performance-based compensation is similar to the value-based model in that the public relations firm only gets paid once results have been achieved. However, the performance model of billing is tied directly to the client's bottom line. Clients only pay for the actual *measureable* increase in business. Compensation is either a share of revenue, cost per action, or a base fee plus a predetermined margin.

Because of metrics easily available on the Internet, this model became quite popular in pricing online marketing and advertising. Concepts such as "cost per thousand" or "cost per mille" (impressions), "cost per click," and "cost per lead" are used to measure performance.[8] Big brands such as Coca-Cola and Procter & Gamble began using this model with their advertisers online and off-line in early 2009 (Chief Marketer Staff 2009, June 8). The increasingly competitive business environment is creating a demand for greater accountability, making this billing model particularly attractive to organizations.

From the client standpoint, the advantage of this pricing model is readily evident; they do not pay for projects or activities that fail to make them money. Clients also appreciate the incentive it gives agencies to leverage the most efficient and effective strategies and channels to produce results. Firm and organization goals tend to be better aligned and firms are motivated to deliver real value. Performance-based pricing also encourages firm integration and cross-pollination of expertise.

While there is some drive to transition to this pricing model, public relations firms generally do not yet use this method. As noted earlier, public relations is still searching for a good method of quantifying results and

---

[8]For definitions of these concepts and terms, refer to Stacks and Bowen (2013).

this model is heavily focused on measuring actual profits as a result of its efforts. Public relations firms are also reluctant to use this model because they have little to no control over the elements of a company's success, such as the company's operating strategy or its image in the marketplace. This model also does not work well for some of the more strategic and non-sales support work that a firm might be brought in to do.

FTE Model

The final billing model discussed here is the *FTE model*. FTE is the number of working hours that represent one full-time employee during a fixed period, such as one month or a year. Firms calculate the number of hours expected to be spent to achieve the client's goals and objectives and convert that workload into the number of people required to complete that work.

Proponents of this model note that having a firm FTE is like having a dedicated employee on staff without the overhead of recruitment and hiring costs, personnel administration costs, and the cost of employee benefits.[9] Clients know they have dedicated resources available to them 24/7. From a procurement viewpoint,[10] the FTE model is a reliable way to measure and quantify a project in specific time increments (days or weeks). It is also a good way for the client to see how the firm expects to deploy resources over a period of time, allowing for more proactive planning to achieve business objectives.[11]

---

[9]http://ebusiness.netsmartz.net/dedicated_resource.asp

[10]As the Council of Public Relations Firms (2011) notes in its report "Public Relations and Procurement," procurement or "strategic sourcing" professionals are increasingly being used to hire public relations firms. To quote the report "Procurement professionals are responsible for helping corporations to enhance the value they receive from outside resources, reduce costs and identify and manage risks associated with outside suppliers." (p. 3)

[11]These benefits directly relate to three of the eight quality management principles outlined in ISO 9004 standards (establishing a process-based quality management system) and are also likely motivators for organizations to involve procurement professionals in the selection of their public relations firm. See: http://www.cnis.gov.cn/wzgg/201111/P020111121513843279516.pdf

Public relations firms generally eschew this billing model because it lacks staffing flexibility to match the variability of work cycles in public relations. It may not be in the client's best interest to pay for an FTE when project loads are light. Finally, it also creates issues in assigning the right person or team with the right skills to the project at the right time; the staff member or team is "locked in" to the client.

Summary

Given all the various billing options, Table 5.1 provides a summary of the billing models. It provides a description of each and addresses each model's advantages and disadvantages.

Table 5.1 Summary of billing models

Billing Model	Description	Advantages	Disadvantages
Hourly Rate	Billed according to time spent on client	• Greater transparency in billing • Easily tracked by firm and client • Value tied directly to objectives • Best for clients requesting specific staff members • Often preferred by procurement experts	• Potential for client to feel "nickel and dimed" • Critics object to paying more for "slow" employees • Creates pressure to take senior people off account • Tends to force work to most junior level • "Clock watching"— client "eats" extra time above contract • Encourages billing for execution not strategy • "Watching the clock" adds stress to client • Potentially inhibits results • Clients also tend to focus on execution not strategy

(continued)

Billing Model	Description	Advantages	Disadvantages
Blended Rate	Similar to hourly, except that hourly rate is used for all employees	• Works well for big teams • Helps balance situations where work is split between junior and senior employees • Provided blended and fair economics to client	• Same as for hourly • Does not provide for ebb and flow of a client's business
Retainer or "Fixed Fee"	Client pays set amount either monthly or annually	• Focus is on output, not time • Puts emphasis on results • Helps clients avoid ebb and flow of PR activities • Simplifies invoicing • Eliminates surprises and contentious billing problems • Provides steady and dependable income for firm • Encourages firm efficiency and high performance	• Potential for both sides to become comfortable and lazy in managing processes and work • Inflexible by nature • Does not reflect vagaries of PR work • Lack of accountability is inherent • Potential for client to demand more effort than budgeted
Value	Results-driven pricing strategy with fee based on predetermined goals and objectives	• Client pays for quantifiable results • Clients guaranteed goals will be met • Fosters a strong relationship between client and firm • Eliminates conflicts of interest built into hourly billing models	• Difficulty defining success • Metrics for increased awareness and changes in attitude difficult to use without significant investment in research • Behavior change difficult to measure and evaluate
Project billing	Set fee for definable activity (e.g., direct mail campaign)	• Most beneficial when tactical elements expensive or involve high out-of-pocket cost activities • Adds flexibility to other billing models when projects emerge, but not defined in Scope of Work	• Not good for building long-term relationships • Some firms use for estimates only, subsequently billing for actual time incurred

Billing Model	Description	Advantages	Disadvantages
Package	Closely resembles project; set fee for packaged or prestructured services (e.g., brand workshop)	• Offers very specific services with specific deliverables • Firm knows precisely the scope of effort • Client knows exactly what they are getting	• Services are often above and beyond those considered part of a retainer arrangement
Performance-Based	Clients only pay for actual measureable increase in business	• Provides greater accountability for client • Client does not pay for projects or activities that fail to make them money • Provides incentives for firms to leverage most efficient strategies and channels • Firm and organization goals tend to be better aligned • Firms motivated to deliver real value • Encourages firm integration and cross-pollination of expertise	• Model is heavily focused on measuring actual profits • Firms still searching for a good method of quantifying results • Firm has little or no control over the elements of a company's success • Does not work well for some of the more strategic and non-sales support work a firm might be asked to do
FTE	Number of working hours that represent one full-time employee during a fixed period	• Like having a dedicated, talented employee on staff without overhead expenses • Clients know they have dedicated resources available 24/7 • From procurement viewpoint, a reliable way to measure and quantify a project • Provides insight to client on how firm expects to deploy resources over time • Allows for more proactive planning to achieve business objectives	• Lacks firm staff flexibility • Doesn't account for variability of work cycles • Very challenging to assign the right person or team with the right skills to the project • Staff member or team "locked in" to the client

Summary

Some experts believe that the hourly pricing model will continue to be the prevalent model used by public relations firms, but that more firms will also offer packaged services. Some opine that a hybrid approach will be used with hourly billing coupled with performance-based incentives added.

It is also likely that public relations firms will move away from the retainer billing model in the future and toward value or performance billing. Agencies want to ensure they are paid for the work that's done and value or performance billing offer compensation for thought and research, not just implementation. These models also offer firms a simplified billing process and allow them to focus on the work at hand. Clients benefit from paying for outcomes rather than time spent working on a project.

That said, moving to performance billing is likely to be a lengthy journey. There is so much a public relations firm accomplishes that may never be measurable, such as internal work, organizational development, counseling of senior management, and preventing crises before they occur. If public relations firms can measure the impact of things that "don't" happen, firms will be able to move fully to a performance-based system. Until then, a blend of billing methods is most likely.

Chapter 6 turns our focus on the specific organization/firm relationship.

PART II

The Working Relationship between Client and Firm

In Part I we introduced the reader to the basics of choosing and working out an agreement with the public relations firm. In particular, we addressed types of public relations firms, what they can and cannot offer, what you should be looking for, what the firm will be doing for you based on agreed scope of the work, and how they expect to be paid. Part II turns to the relationship a client and firm have after an initial decision is made to offer the firm a contract. In Chapter 6 the general expectations of the client–firm relationship is explored. Chapter 7 then looks at how the firm should keep the client informed as it works through the scope of work and offers updates at specified times in the campaign or program. Chapter 8 explores the execution of the public relations firm's activities and Chapter 9 looks at how the firm should evaluate its activities, the success of those activities (campaign or program), and whether the firm's actions met the client's expected return on investment (ROI).

CHAPTER 6

The Client–Firm Relationship

The relationship with our public relations firm is very tight. They are always on top of issues that we are facing, decisions being made and offer great insight and counsel. Their objectivity is what we value most.
—CEO, Private University

We started slow, involving them in a project or two. When we realized how valuable their counsel was to all aspects of the operation, they became an integral part of the team.
—VP, Public Relations, Health Care

We find that we can build trust of our counsel inside an organization by starting a relationship with interviews that put us next to each member of senior management. We then understand their individual views and goals along with how they work with their colleagues. It allows us to build trust across the management team and negotiate the landmines that are always in place.
—Partner, Public Relations Firm

Our relationships with public relations firms are much more vendor-oriented. We do RFPs that establish exactly what is to be done and they do it with very little pushback. They do not become part of the "team". It works for us but sometimes I wonder what we may be missing.
—Director of Public Affairs, Municipal Utility

In the previous chapters, we addressed the need for a relationship between the organization, you, and the public relations firm you chose to work with on some problem or opportunity. But what exactly does that mean? Are there different kinds of relationships? Which are most successful? What sorts of interaction should be seen in an excellent relationship?

Obviously, an important aspect of getting the most out of your public relations firm is how well the client/firm association comes together and how strong it is. A good relationship is important for both firm and client; the firm wishes to retain clients by helping them achieve their goals and objectives and the client wishes to successfully achieve those goals and objectives so as to drive their business forward. A flawed, failing, or failed relationship damages both parties. In addition to revenue loss, the firm loses major investments in time and effort and potentially, reputation. The failure to build a long-lasting, healthy relationship for the client results in failure to achieve goals and objectives and probably loss of revenue. This also causes significant additional investment in time and money on the client's part finding a new partnership, a process that can take months or years.

This chapter discusses the difference between a strategic and a vendor relationship, focusing on the advantages of a *strategic partnership*. We will discuss important aspects of a strategic relationship. We will also discuss firm and client expectations within the relationship, the importance of communication, access to senior management, and the optimal relationship between the firm and the internal public relations function.

Agency vs. Firm

In our Introduction, we advanced the idea that the term "agency" suggested that the relationship with a public relations counsel was a vendor relationship, offering a product that is interchangeable with others offering the same product. We also opined that like an organization's relationship with its attorneys, the professional services offered by a public relations firm was *counsel*, not a product.

Look at this distinction in more detail. Your organization hires a vendor to provide a specific product or service, such as copy paper, ink toner, or maintenance of your fleet of vehicles. Printing services are also often considered vendors.

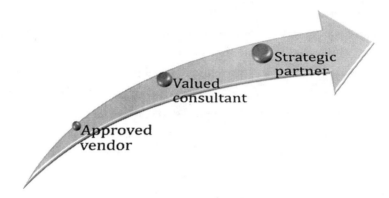

Figure 6.1 The path to a successful firm/client relationship

Vendors provide products and service solutions important to the success of your organization. They become valued consultants when they also offer functional capabilities and tactical initiatives. When the two entities share common goals and develop and enact mutual strategies to meet those goals, a strategic partnership is formed (see Figure 6.1).

As a noun, the word "counsel" means "the act of exchanging opinions and ideas" or "consultation." It also means "advice or guidance, especially as solicited from a knowledgeable person" (http://www.thefreedictionary.com/counsel). Likewise, advice means to provide an "opinion about what could or should be done about a situation or problem" (http://www.thefreedictionary.com/advice).

Thus, the relationship with the organization's public relations firm will be most successful as a *strategic* partnership where client and firm collaborate to find solutions to business problems or challenges. Public relations is ineffective and the partnership will be unsuccessful when the firm is expected to simply be "order takers."

Trust and Mutual Understanding

At the heart of any relationship is *trust*. The client needs to trust that the firm knows what it is doing, particularly if the client has done its due diligence as described in Chapter 3 and *vice versa*. Building trust in a relationship requires an appreciation for the expertise of the other party. Both client and firm need to recognize the strengths each party brings to the relationship. Focusing on the "but" or what you would change as a client or firm does not engender trust on the part of the other. There are times when we simply need to defer to the expertise that is not our own.

In order for there to be a great partnership, it is absolutely essential that there be *mutual understanding*. Both client and firm need to invest the time and effort *at the beginning* to truly understand each other. Energy invested early in getting to know one another—people, facilities, history, aspirations, issues, and so forth—will return manyfold with future success. The firm should be committed to knowing the client's business and the industry inside out. A firm that immerses themselves in their client asks a ton of questions about what has worked and not worked in the past. The deeper this understanding, the greater chance there is for great ideas that add value, the less risk there is in challenging norms and the greater opportunity to build the business in new and exciting ways. What is important at this stage is that the client and firm have established a mutual dialogue that continues throughout the relationship and provides the basis for how disagreements can be discussed in an open and supportive climate.

Deep understanding like this also comes from knowing the people involved in the organization. Firms should be intent on finding out what the client really thinks about the challenges the organization is facing. Understanding what the executives think their reputation is in the marketplace can provide an exceptional starting point for all involved. To truly understand what matters, the firm needs to know what keeps the client up at night.

Goals and Expectations

An indispensable part of this mutual understanding is shared goals and expectations. Both client and firm need to hammer out common objectives and their measures up front. In the process, the client has to be willing to share all available data and business documents with the firm, including marketing and strategic business plans, so the firm can see where their efforts fit into the bigger picture. The firm likewise needs to share its perspective and knowledge of the industry and market landscape as well as the legislative, media, and stakeholder environment.

The firm absolutely has to understand the client's priorities, timing, budget, and other constraints. The firm should not promise or agree to results that are highly unlikely just to win the business. At the same time, the client needs to understand the reality of their situation and what kinds of results are feasible and realistic. Being honest with each other from the beginning is the key to compatible expectations. It is especially important for the firm to have the guts to say "no" to a bad idea or outrageous request, doing so diplomatically, of course. If the firm's focus is on keeping the client happy, they are setting the client up for major disappointment later. Education and clarity about what is and is not reasonable goes a long way toward creating more of the most essential element in a relationship—trust.

Anticipating and Handling Risk and Failure

Another important element of a great relationship is how risk and failure are handled. Things are not always going to go as planned. Clients who are truly committed to success understand that there is always risk in searching for great ideas. Rather than asking the firm to shoulder all that risk themselves, they accept the idea that with great risk comes great reward and agree to share in the risk to arrive at outstanding work. The firm knows the client has their back and that they are totally in it together. Great clients hold themselves and their firm accountable for the quality and success of the end product and share in the responsibility of "getting it right."

On the flip side, firms have to guard against complacency and becoming "risk averse." They should never allow their people to stagnate over a piece of business or fail to challenge the status quo. Sometimes firms have to risk the turbulence that comes with bringing in fresh people with new ideas, if that is what it takes to push the envelope. The best firms actively avoid the trap of giving the client what they will buy or think they want rather than the strategies they need.

As with any relationship that matters, how disagreements are handled is extremely important. The mere fact there is disagreement should not be cause for concern, especially if that disagreement is driven by the passion of both sides to succeed. What is important is how that disagreement is handled. After all, as General George Patton famously said, "If everyone is thinking alike, someone isn't thinking" (http://www.brainyquote.com/quotes/quotes/g/georgespa130444.html).

Open and Honest Exchange

As noted earlier, a thriving partnership values open and honest exchange of concerns. Being reticent about bringing up questions related to performance or expectations until they become a real problem is a formula for disaster. The faster this discussion takes place, the faster course corrections can be made and the faster the program can get back on track. In the process both parties need to remember the *Golden Rule* and treat each other as they themselves want to be treated.

Being patient may be one of the hardest elements in a relationship, but an extremely important one. We all want partnerships that hit the ground running and produce instant results. This becomes increasingly critical as future generations move into the business world with their expectations of and experience with instant gratification. Sometimes, the firm just needs to be patient and try and understand the timing of client decisions. Knowing the inner workings of the client's organization well is a good antidote to impatience caused by this situation.

On the other hand, the client needs to be patient with the timing of the firm's delivery of results. A front page, above-the-fold story in the *New York Times* is not something that occurs each time the firm releases something and may, in fact, never happen unless the release covers something truly newsworthy. Positive trends over time and keeping an eye on the end result are what we should be looking for throughout the course of the campaign.

Importance of Good Communication

A common thread running throughout all of the previous discussion is the importance of communication, but it is worth a quick focus here. The most successful client–firm relationships are those where the communication is *open and transparent*. True fidelity in a relationship is the result of clear and frequent communication. Today's technology makes it easy to stay in touch—a short email here, a quick text there. But personal and one-on-one communication should never be overlooked in our technologically advanced world. There is nothing better than picking up the phone and talking, or better yet catching up face-to-face, to build a strong relationship.

This verbal connection also establishes a trust factor. Frequent communication—open and faithful communication—helps eliminate misinterpretations, misunderstanding, and mistakes. This is particularly true if the time is taken and commitment is made to build multiple communication channels, both formal and informal, between the client and the firm. Clients and firms who allow for "back channel" communication (behind the scenes discussion) for testing ideas and gathering information find a richer, more robust and successful relationship.

Communication like this can create a sense of *esprit de corps* and camaraderie that encourages the expenditure of more energy on the part of both. The best firms also use this communication principle to show the client that they are always thinking about their business, offering up ideas, anticipating needs, and going above and beyond. Ideally, this communication includes celebrating successes, personal and business. A good rule of thumb is to have a phone conversation with your firm at least once a week and an in-person meeting at least once a quarter.

Access to Management

Access to and attention from senior-level executives whenever and wherever necessary is a *sine qua non* of a successful client–firm relationship. Things work best when the firm offers its most senior members when the situation calls for it and sometimes when it does not. Clients will feel more confident and comfortable in their relationship with the firm when they know that the most experienced members of the firm are paying attention to their campaign.

Likewise, you need to make sure you are offering the firm access to the right people and information. Nothing stifles success—or is more frustrating for all involved—than gatekeepers, well-meaning or otherwise, preventing direct contact with firm members or creating additional layers of approval and/or delivery of information. In a similar vein, the client must make every effort to ensure all personnel make responding to the agency a priority and understand the importance of doing so.

Finally, where an internal public relations function exists, great care should be taken to include at least representatives of that staff in *every* meeting involving the firm. The fast track to disaster is creating a situation where the internal public relations staff feels devalued or excluded. The success of your relationship with a firm is directly proportional to the extent to which the internal team feels an equal partner in the collaboration and decision making (see Figure 6.2).[1]

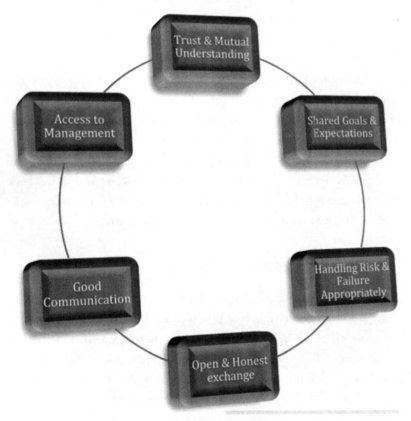

Figure 6.2 Elements of an outstanding relationship with your public relations firm

---

[1] A major limitation that firms often face is a lack of knowledge about the problems they are called in to solve. In instances where there is an internal public relations function, the people in that function can and should provide background information that may not be evident regarding the problem. This client–firm relationship is important to bring the firm up to speed regarding prior events and also to not make the same mistake.

Summary

It should be apparent at this point that the best relationship between you and your firm is one that is strategic in nature, based on trust and mutual understanding with shared goals and expectations. Good communication, open and honest exchanges, and access to top management are essential parts of this formula for success. One of the hardest, but most important, parts of a great relationship is how the two parties handle risk and failure. Not everything is going to go exactly as planned. If firm and client are truly committed to success, they have each other's backs and understand that the greater the risk the greater the reward. Finally, disagreements are a part of every relationship. Handled appropriately, they lead to even greater success. Peter Drucker (1967), in his seminal work *The Effective Executive*, went so far as to say "The understanding that underlies the right decision grows out of the clash and conflict of divergent opinions and out of the serious consideration of competing alternatives" (p. 143). These then are the keys to an excellent relationship.

We'll next discuss an important part of managing the work once it has begun: progress reports.

CHAPTER 7

Progress Reports[1]

Once the work has begun an important part of managing the process is reporting on progress. These progress reports come in many formats (e.g., memo, interview, and short note accompanying the invoice) and are customizable based on your needs. Some clients do not feel the need for these reports, but if the company is not getting regular updates from the firm, you are not getting the feedback needed from your public relations firm. After all, they were presumably hired to accomplish something important to your business objectives. Just as financial reports help understand the financial health of the business, a progress report from a public relations firm will help keep you up to speed on the health of your public relations effort.

What information should you expect in a progress report? The answer really depends on the situation, but generally progress reports should provide the following information:

1. *Background on the project itself:* This section may not be necessary if the firm is providing frequent reports, but can be especially important if you are only requiring quarterly or annual reports. The public relations firm should take a paragraph or two to refresh you on the nature of the project, the agreed upon objectives, and what the status of the work/project was at the time of last reporting.

[1]**Acknowledgment:** The authors would like to thank Debbie Schramm, president, and Lindsey Laird, vice president, Saxum, Debbie Anglin, principal, Anglin PR, Brenda Jones Barwick, president, Jones PR, and Blake Lewis, principal, Lewis Public Relations, for their assistance in providing input for this chapter. We hope these examples will help you determine what kind of progress reports you'd like so you can get the most out of your public relations firm.

2. *Discussion of achievements since last report:* If this report is on a specific project or campaign, this section should provide an update of the firm's progress on the tasks presented in the project schedule. If the firm is on retainer, this section should outline all of the work done by the firm along with the results of that effort. These reports can focus on outputs alone or outputs and outtakes, outputs and outcomes, or all three (please see Chapter 10 for a discussion on the distinction between the three). Enclosures or attachments to the report should provide evidence of this progress in the form of media clips and other relevant documents.

3. *Discussion of problems that have arisen:* While we all hope the public relations firm's effort has been without difficulties, it is also important to allow your public relations counsel the opportunity to share or warn you about problems that have arisen or could appear on the horizon. This allows you to provide a possible solution, if you have one. At the very least, this provides an opportunity to collaborate with you on a solution.

3. *Discussion of work that lies ahead:* The firm should provide you with an outline of how it will meet your objectives in the short term. If this report is related specifically to a project or campaign, this section should walk through what remains to be done in the plan of action contained in the original plan.

To illustrate the variety of approaches to progress reports, the authors interviewed several public relations firm principals on their reporting practices. SAXUM, an integrated marketing communication firm based in Oklahoma City, Oklahoma, requires all account managers to provide detailed monthly reports, as well as an annual report to retainer clients outlining the previous year's highlights and achievements and *key performance indicators* (KPIs) that relate directly to the clients' objectives. In addition, the firm evaluates client satisfaction through interview and survey methods. Saxum's top 10 clients receive a one-on-one telephone interview with a third party and the rest of their clients receive an online survey. The research findings are developed by the SAXUM team and the third party. According to Saxum president Debbie Schramm (2013, July 23), "Client satisfaction surveys are an important aspect of our business and reporting process. We can get caught up checking tactics off the list, but by having a designated time when we ask our clients about overall performance, we often reveal insights we would have otherwise never known."

Examples of both data gathering forms are found in Figures 7.1 and 7.2. The phone interviews are customized before the call following interviews with the account manager. They are in the process of developing end-of-project reviews as well.

Debbie Anglin, APR, principal of Anglin PR in Oklahoma City, Oklahoma, provides progress reports based on the scope and timing of projects (Anglin 2013, June 27). Larger, longer term projects get *interim* reports. Other clients get a *final* report upon completion of the project. The information contained in each report varies greatly, depending on what they are doing for the client. They typically provide clients with:

- An overview (like a restatement of their scope or what they said they will deliver in their contract);
- The tactics employed with quantities where appropriate (i.e., number of people called, blogs written, media outlets pitched, and so forth);
- The outcomes/results of their efforts in quantitative *and* qualitative measures wherever possible;
- "Next steps" in a bulleted format;
- Any "musings;" and
- Things that went well or that were a hindrance or new information uncovered.

Anglin also told us, "We find our reports are just as helpful for us as they are for our clients over the history of the account." She also noted that they write their reports in a way that their clients can use all or pieces of the report to create any reports the client has to provide others (e.g., leadership, partners/collaborators, investors, and board members). She went on to say, "They are so important in demonstrating value and ROI [Return on Investment] that we bring. They are time-consuming for us to create, but certainly "make the case" for why they hired us."

SAXUM

1. Let's start with a background question. Would you tell me which of Saxum's services your organization currently employs?
   - Advertising and Creative Services
   - Digital
   - Public Relations

2. Now I'd ask you to think about Saxum's performance and rate it when it comes to a number of important qualities using the scale of *excellent, very good, good, fair, or poor*. And please distinguish if you give different Saxum rankings for different services. Let's start with strategy. How would you rate Saxum when it comes to strategy?
   - Strategy
   - Creativity
   - Trust
   - Execution of initiatives
   - Knowledge of your industry
   - Responsiveness/accessibility

3. Now I'd ask you to consider the same qualities and rank how important they are to you when evaluating an integrated communications agency. I'd ask you to use the criteria of *extremely important, very important, important, somewhat important, and not important*. Again, please note any difference in the importance among services that Saxum provides. Let's start once more with strategy.
   - Strategy
   - Creativity
   - Trust
   - Execution of initiatives
   - Knowledge of your industry
   - Responsiveness/accessibility

4. I'd like to dig a little deeper on the quality of Saxum's work.
   - Would you be able to give me some specific examples of very good work by Saxum, including our interaction with your Saxum team, and why you think it went well?
   - And likewise, would you tell me about areas where you think Saxum performance has not been as strong? Please include details about the team and the situation.
   - Would you describe for me the level of leadership that you feel Saxum's management team provides your organization?
   - And, in general, how do you describe the value you receive from Saxum?

5. Is there anything about your relationship with Saxum or their work that I haven't asked you that you would like to comment on?

6. Given your experience with Saxum, how likely are you to recommend Saxum to another organization? (Probe for Yes or No.) Why is that?

7. Would you like a senior member of the Saxum team to contract you to discuss your evaluation of the agency?
   - Yes
   - No

Figure 7.1 One-on-one interview. Used with permission of Saxum

SAXUM

The following provides questions for the Saxum client satisfaction survey incorporating the consultant's recommendations and subsequent revisions.

Introduction

Welcome! Saxum is committed to providing our clients with the best integrated marketing communications services. The information you share with us about your experience with Saxum will help us continue to enhance the work we do. Important details of the survey are included below. Thank you for taking a few minutes to answer our questions.

Sincerely,

Renzi Stone, Chairman & CEO   Debbie Schramm, President

Evaluation details:

- The estimated completion time is about 5 minutes.
- Please be honest and forthcoming.
- If you have technical questions regarding the evaluation, please contact Kate Cunningham, marketing insights fellow, at 405.605.2003 or kcunningham@saxum.com

Questionnaire

1. Based on your experience with Saxum, how would you rate the performance of Saxum in the following areas? (format: rating matrix; "excellent" to "poor")
   - Strategy
   - Creativity
   - Trust
   - Execution of initiatives
   - Knowledge of your industry
   - Responsiveness/accessibility

2. How would you rank the following qualities in terms of how important they are to you when considering an integrated communications agency? (format: rating scale; "extremely important" to "not important at all")
   - Strategy
   - Creativity
   - Trust
   - Execution of initiatives
   - Knowledge of your industry
   - Responsiveness/accessibility

3. How satisfied are you with your account team? (format: rating scale; "extremely satisfied" to "not satisfied at all")

4. Please take a moment to explain your rating of your account team. Feel free to reference specific team members or examples.
   - Blank field

5. How likely are you to recommend Saxum to another organization? (format: multiple choice)

Figure 7.2 Online survey. Used with permission of Saxum

SAXUM

- Extremely likely
- Very likely
- Neither likely nor unlikely
- Somewhat unlikely
- Not likely at all

6. How satisfied are you with the value you receive from Saxum? (format: rating scale; "extremely satisfied" to "not satisfied at all")

7. Please take a moment to discuss your rating from the question above.
    - Blank field

8. Please verify your professional email address. (format: comment box)
    - Blank field

9. Which of Saxum's services does your organization currently employ? Please select all that apply. (format: multiple choice)
    - Advertising and Creative Services
    - Digital
    - Public Relations

10. Would you like a senior member of the Saxum team to contact you to discuss your evalution of the agency? (format: multiple choice)
    - Yes
    - No

Exit to Saxum homepage.

Figure 7.2 (Continued)

Anglin PR also provides a summarized version on their invoice, because they have found many times that a different person sees/processes the invoice than the person they routinely work with. "We feel like the summary helps the person better understand the charges," Anglin said.

Brenda Jones Barwick, APR, president of Jones PR in Oklahoma City, Oklahoma, provides a variety of progress reports, again dependent on the client. Their reports vary, but typically fall into one of two categories; the *media report* and the *task report*. Barwick (2013, July 2) noted that:

Media reports are especially helpful during an important media event, like a new product launch, an important news item being released, etc. Task reports typically showcase our efforts, which in turn shows the client what they're paying for. Although the client may see results in media hits, it's also nice for them to see what efforts we took to get those hits.

For one of their larger clients, Verizon Wireless, Jones PR provides a report on a weekly basis that includes both a weekly task report and a media report of coverage secured during the previous week. In addition to their weekly reports for Verizon, they send a monthly report that combines the task report and the media report to provide an overall snapshot of the month. This report also includes values, Barwick said, "estimated earned values and estimated audience reach."

The biggest report Jones PR generates is the *annual review*. They use a presentation format rather than an actual report, showcasing some of the biggest highlights of the year. They often are accompanied with multimedia, photos of media clips, and statistics on hits during the year before and the current year.

Typically at Jones PR, the person creating the report works directly on the account. The task of reporting is done by an account coordinator or assistant account executive and then reviewed and approved by a senior account executive or vice president, depending on the scale of the report. A weekly report would likely be reviewed by the account executive while an annual overview would be reviewed by a vice president.

Blake Lewis, III, APR, Fellow PRSA, principal, Lewis Public Relations in Dallas, Texas, told us that reports are provided on a client-by-client basis, depending on what they want and/or what the firm believes they need.

> More sophisticated clients who are buying us for bandwidth often can see the level of progress and prefer that all of our resources be invested in market-facing work; others whom we may feel are less able to see work product and outcomes without some alerting activity will get reports, regardless of their desires (Lewis 2013, June 27).

He went on to note that, "Our focus is on results, right down to the name—not 'Activity Report' or 'Progress Report,' but, rather, 'Results and Activities Report.' These generally are issued on a monthly basis."

The information Lewis and his team provide their clients includes what was accomplished (outcomes versus goals and objectives), evidence of the work that drove those outcomes (outputs such as clips, other relevant documents), and a list of intermediate activities that either led to the outcomes or are focused on achieving outcomes in the subsequent reporting period. "These reports also provide [an advance look at] work being conducted in the beginnings of the next reporting period as a form of preview" (Lewis 2013, June 27). The account staff generally produce the reports, but all are reviewed/approved by a staff leader in the agency before distribution to their clients.

Summary

As evidenced by the discussion above, we suggest looking at progress reports as not just a way for the public relations firm to report on its activities and results. They should be viewed as a way to build a tighter relationship between client and firm. Progress reports help create transparency into the advancement of the client's public relations objectives. This transparency should build trust on both sides and more confidence in what is gotten from investment in the firm's abilities to track and solve the challenge for which it was hired. These reports should also provide the client with competitive insights and help you and your firm determine whether or not your public relations strategy is appropriate. In partnership with your firm, you are much better positioned to make adjustments if you are tracking the progress of your public relations efforts.

In the following chapter (Chapter 8), we will discuss the various elements of the actual execution of the work.

CHAPTER 8

Research and Execution

This chapter presumes that the client and the firm have agreed to a defined Scope of Work and are ready to begin their relationship. Now it is time for the firm to more closely examine the specific problems that are affecting the organization and plan specifics for achieving the goals set forth. In this chapter we discuss the core steps your firm should take to prepare a detailed and thoughtful plan of action to achieve the established goals.

However, given the unpredictable nature of the world, there will always be unexpected situations that require an immediate response. Yet that response should also follow a rigorous (though truncated) methodology that assures you have the best approach to the situation at hand. Much of the material that follows is applicable in formulating responses to both scenarios.

At the heart of every public relations campaign or program, at least in terms of best practices, is *a continuous four-step process*. This four-step process is known by a plethora of different acronyms: RPIE, RACE, PPAE, and so forth. Simply stated, the four-step process includes:

1. Research,
2. Planning or analysis,
3. Implementation/execution/communication, and
4. Evaluation.

Allen Center and Pat Jackson (2003, p. 14), both pioneers in strategic communication planning with a focus on behavioral outcomes, present the best description of the process:

1. *Fact-finding and data gathering*: Defining the problem, challenge, or opportunity; often includes formal research.

2. *Planning and programming*: Developing and packaging the actual plan itself.
3. *Action, relationship building, and communication*: The actual implementation of the plan.
4. *Evaluation*: Determining the results and deciding what to do next or differently.

Other books also give excellent overviews of the process. Chapter Nine of the Bowen et al. (2010) work included in this Public Relations Collection titled *An Overview of the Public Relations Function* covers this process in great detail. An excellent primer on *public relations research* is contained in Michaelson & Stacks' *A Professional and Practitioner's Guide to Public Relations Research, Measurement and Evaluation* (2014), also in this collection. Therefore, it would be unnecessary to have an in-depth discussion of the four-step process in this volume. There are, however, a number of areas within the four steps that deserve extra focus.

The Process

Two extremely important outcomes of the research step important to the discussion on execution are goals and objectives. Once sufficient data has been gathered so that client and firm *truly* understand the problem, challenge, or opportunity at the fundamental causal level, the campaign or program's *goals* can be created (or modified). Goals provide the direction of the plan and, obviously, reflect the overall business goals of your organization. They are "a *projected* outcome that is desired" (Michaelson and Stacks 2014, p. 37). As expectations, goals are devoid of specific measurement and are fairly general. A goal might be to *pass a bond to support the school budget, gain zoning approval for plant expansion,* or *rebuild trust and customer loyalty after a crisis.*

At this point, client and firm should review the goals outlined in the Scope of Work document (see Chapter 4) and ensure they are still valid given the additional data provided by the firm's research. It may be that the research shows that the problem, challenge, or opportunity exists in an entirely different plane than first suspected. Rigidly adhering to the Scope of Work as written would be foolish in the face of such evidence.

Revising the Scope of Work early in the planning process typically should not alter the cost of the campaign or program unless the situation revealed is much more complex than anticipated.

The specific, measurable outcomes necessary to achieve these goals are listed as objectives in the plan. Stacks (2011, p. 340) defines objectives as "an explicit statement [or statements] that support(s) a communication strategy." Bowen et al. (2010) set four criteria for a good objective:

1. It should be an end and not a means to an end; an outcome that contributes to the goal.
2. It should be measurable; comparative number or **benchmark** set against a **baseline** (more on this below).
3. It should have a time frame; when the objective will be accomplished.
4. It should identify the public for which the outcome is intended.

As we noted in Chapter 4, every goal must have at least three objectives: (1) informational; (2) motivational; and (3) behavioral. They are sequential and based on the way we learn. Note though that Pat Jackson (in pr reporter, 7-30-90, 8-30-90, 11-4-96) also discussed the fact that motivation can often follow behavior rather than precede it. Getting a stakeholder to practice a behavior—even if they do not agree with it attitudinally—can result in a position shift because cognitive dissonance (Festinger 1957) forces humans to reconcile their attitudes to support and defend their behaviors.) Regardless, it is important in the context of the four-step process to delve into each more deeply.

Informational objectives specify what stakeholders should know during and after the campaign or program. This objective is sometimes referred to as an "awareness" objective. Stakeholders with little or no knowledge of your organization need to be provided with information so they can be alert to the campaign or program. Even those stakeholders who are already active with the campaign or program need to be provided this information as they may have misconceptions or be ignorant of certain information, which might influence the way they feel and/or act. Informational objectives specify the knowledge known or needed by the stakeholders for whom the campaign is intended along with the channels used and how they will be used (Stacks 2011, p. 28).

Motivational objectives relate to the attitudes of stakeholders. As Stacks (2011) points out, "an attitude can be seen as possessing direction (like/dislike), salience (importance/unimportance), and understanding (ignorance/understanding)" (p. 28). Once people possess information about the campaign, they will naturally begin to develop an attitude, positive or negative, toward the campaign. Motivational objectives test the effect of the information provided as well as the intention or potential to behave in a certain manner.

Of ultimate importance to you and your organization are the *behavioral objectives*. Sometimes called "action" or "outcome" objectives, this is the actual response or action by the stakeholders targeted in the campaign. Behavioral objectives are the decisive end state that defines the success or failure of the campaign. If the response or action is what was intended, the campaign is a success. Otherwise, the campaign did not achieve what it was designed to achieve (Stacks 2011, p. 29).

David Michaelson (Michaelson and Stacks 2011) takes a slightly different approach to objectives in what he calls the BASIC model of the Communication Life Cycle (see Figure 8.1). His argument is that all communication objectives need to be tied to understanding where a public or target audience is in the life cycle of a communication event. If there is no awareness of objective, then you must first build awareness. If there is awareness, then you would advance knowledge. Both of these

- **BASIC** communication objectives for public relations efforts:
  - ○ **B**uild awareness
  - ○ **A**dvance knowledge
  - ○ **S**ustain relevance
  - ○ **I**nitiate action
  - ○ **C**reate advocacy

Figure 8.1 The communication life cycle. Used with permission

objectives are informational. Sustaining relevance and initiating action are motivational objectives, they seek to providers to move the target audience or public to some behavior; thus, they are motivational objectives. Finally, you want behavior—in most public relations cases this is to get others to promote what you are promoting, thus distancing you from the problem or goal; this has been called "third-party endorsement" (Stacks and Michaelson 2009) and the creating of advocacy reflects the behavioral objective.

Strategy and Planning

It is important to understand objectives as they have a tremendous impact on the other three steps of the four-step process, especially evaluation. Once the goal(s) and measurable objectives have been formulated, the next step in the public relations campaign is *planning*. A critical task early in the planning phase is identifying strategies as they relate to each objective. *Goals are the direction, objectives the destinations, and strategy is the plan to get there.* Strategy takes into consideration all the theoretical underpinnings surrounding human nature that are known to move behavior. In public relations, strategies direct the "big ideas" and key themes and messages for the campaign or program. As Bowen et al. (2010, p. 95) discuss, four specific elements need to be included in developing strategies.

> First, *identify* what is trying to be accomplished with each public [stakeholder] (tie the strategy to an objective). Second, *segment audiences [stakeholders]* based on common characteristics. Third, *create* communication strategies that are focused on the self-awareness of the public [stakeholders]. And, fourth, identify how public [stakeholders] will be *reached* with messages or actions.

Tactics

Flowing from the strategies are the specific steps needed to complete each. These specific steps or tools and tasks are the *tactics* (outputs) and can be the most creative element of the planning stage. Here the public relations firm will come up with the messages, designs, and activities that will allow accomplishment of each strategy and objective (Bowen et al. 2010, pp. 97–98).

Implementation

Once the plan is written, it is then *implemented*, which is step three of the four-step process. The best public relations campaigns or programs focus on communication *and* action, because actions must follow words as it must in all business disciplines. Sometimes, words are not enough and the organization must make changes to its actions or reactions in order for the communication to be effective. For instance, if employees are not using the intranet for information it might not be enough to redesign the site. It may require that the site contain more relevant information for employees or be more interesting to them. Just because the organization wants stakeholders to act a certain way will not make it so. Sometimes the organization needs to change its way of operating to improve the relationship (Bowen et al. 2010, p. 28).

During the planning phase, two important elements of implementation are developed; the *timeline* or *plan of action* and milestones and the *budget*. More attention will be given to each in Chapter 9, but both provide a road map for the client and firm as the campaign and plan are implemented. The timeline need not be overly sophisticated as long as it establishes deadlines and important milestones. Many firms use Gantt or PERT charts (see Figures 8.2 and 8.3) to develop their plan of action and

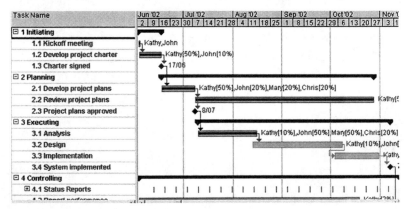

Figure 8.2 Example of a Gantt chart

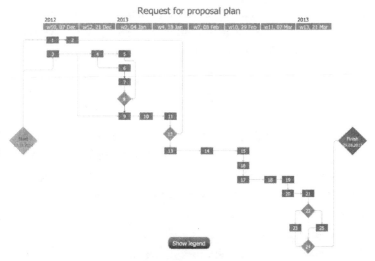

Figure 8.3 Example of PERT chart

milestones and most agency management software includes a similar tool (Bowen et al. 2010, p. 98).

Similarly, the budget will capture the costs of creating, distributing, and executing the tactics; including personnel, material, media costs, equipment and facilities, and administrative items such as postage, delivery, printing, and so forth. In best practice, the budget has been on the table from the beginning. During the planning phase, client and firm consider the level of expenditure necessary to achieve goals and objectives and determined what was reasonable. Implementation is crunch time and the campaign or program must be executed within those parameters. The three key principles of public relations budgeting are it must be *realistic, practical, and "doable."*

Evaluation

Step four is *evaluation,* which will also be discussed in greater detail in the following chapter. That said, there are two critical elements of any evaluation that are executed during the implementation phase as well as the conclusion of the campaign. These elements are *baselines* and *benchmarks*. While many people use the two terms interchangeably, they are significantly different and individually critical to determining not only the ultimate success or failure of the campaign or program, but help refine, re-center or refocus the campaign's activities by allowing the effectiveness of the implementation of those activities to be tested during the execution phase.

Baseline

The *baseline* of the campaign or project ties directly back to the objectives and provides the starting point from which the impact of every subsequent action/activity is measured. According to Michaelson and Stacks (2014), baselines are established during the *formative research phase* (research done before the campaign or project) conducted in step one of the four-step process. Formative research seeks to measure pre-campaign levels of awareness, attitudes, perceptions, stakeholder needs, and the like. Absent a baseline, it is impossible to identify whether or not any progress is made. For example, how can you tell your stakeholders attitudes toward your environmental record have changed if you have not measured what they were before the campaign or program started?

Benchmarks

Benchmarks are the hoped-for, incremental advances that should appear over time during the campaign or project. These projected targets for accomplishment should be established during the planning phase and used to test the plan's effectiveness throughout the campaign. Just as in every other business discipline, measurement along the way helps establish and evaluate campaign effectiveness and allows for adjustments to the plan along the way. If everything is on phase and on target, we continue to execute the plan as written. If we miss a target, we adjust and refine the plan to account for and overcome the shortfall. Benchmarks provide important feedback regarding the plan, tactics, and outtakes (Stacks 2011).

This kind of evaluation of business and communication goals provides the necessary feedback needed for accurate and successful decision making. If the communication content (outputs, explained in detail on Chapter 10) is not getting out, not being retained, or is being retained but recalled in error, you and your firm should decide to revise or modify the plan. If the communication content is being received and understood, you and your firm will need to determine whether or not their attitudes are changing or being reinforced. Finally, you and your firm will need to decide whether your desired stakeholders are likely to doing what you want them to do and/or actually doing it. A fuller discussion of this sort of *evaluative research* follows in Chapter 9.

There is often a temptation when working with a public relations firm to shortchange both formative and evaluative research. In the dozen or so major surveys on research and evaluation in public relations conducted over the past 20 years, the major reasons for failing to conduct research or evaluation remain essentially the same; it is too expensive, it is not wanted, or it is too time-intensive.

Do not be tempted to cut back on these important elements of execution and evaluation. As Peter Drucker (1954, p. 351) famously declared, "The most serious mistakes are not being made as a result of wrong answers. The true dangerous thing is asking the wrong question." Unless research is invested before, during, and after the campaign you may well be putting into action a plan that addresses the wrong question(s).

Likewise, he also said, "There is surely nothing quite so useless, as doing with great efficiency, something that should not be done at all" (Drucker 2003, p. 64). No amount of effort or elegance of execution will achieve the desired effect if you are not doing what you need to be doing to solve the problem, seize the initiative, or meet the challenge your organization faces. Only the kind of feedback that results from continuous measurement and evaluation will allow you to make those decisions critical to the achievement of your business and communication objectives.

Summary

Public relations is a process, a continuous series of deliberate actions taken in sequence with the intent to cause a positive change in something, be it awareness, intent to purchase, or a behavior. The process is iterative with each step overlapping the other. Because the process involves continuous measurement and evaluation, it is flexible allowing for adjustment when necessary.

Chapter 9 will focus more closely on the evaluation phase of public relations planning.

CHAPTER 9

Evaluation

By creating measureable goals at the outset of our work together, it was easy to gauge the success of the work the firm had done for us. In turn, that gave me the data I needed to justify our budgets for the following year!

—Director of Public Relations, Public University

The research tools we used at the beginning of the project to ascertain the organization's challenges were the same tools we used at the end to measure success.

—VP, Public Relations, Utility

We used evaluation tools throughout the project to tweak strategy and messaging in order to stay on course. By the end of the project we knew how far we had come from our baseline marks. It actually didn't take much more to finalize the numbers and use them in reporting on our success

—Director, Public Relations, Insurance Company

Once the client's goals and objectives are finalized in collaboration with the public relations firm, you essentially have established the criteria by which you would evaluate the success of your campaign or program. Evaluation begins by *correlating* public relations outcomes with business outcomes to establish the effectiveness and true Return on Investment (ROI) of the public relations function.

It is also important to note that establishing a best practices plan will show that evaluation is not considered useful *only* in determining success or failure, but in how the communication effort can be changed and improved to be even more effective in the future.

Ongoing evaluation of the *entirety of your public relations efforts* can also result in identifying various "nonfinancial indicators" as part of what Patrick Jackson (1997, p. 1) called the "double bottom line." Beyond the public relations function's contribution to the *financial* bottom line is its importance to *reputational* bottom line, which includes outcomes associated with both organizational effectiveness and public policy (see Chapter 1). An organization's social responsibility activities, issue anticipation and crisis management, change agent activities, and work to overcome executive isolation—all public relations responsibilities—contribute to a smoother path for achieving all organizational goals and have become identified as *nonfinancial indicators* of business success or failure (Stacks 2011; Michaelson and Stacks 2014). Their impact should be measured and reported in the same breath as financial indicators to gain a complete picture of the public relation's function value.

A very through and excellent explanation of public relations research and measurement, including campaign evaluation, is contained in *A Professional and Practitioner's Guide to Public Relations Research, Measurement, and Evaluation*, another of the Public Relations Collection works by David Michaelson and Don Stacks; hence this chapter will focus on those elements most important to you in evaluating whether or not you are getting the most out of your public relations firm.

Baselines and Benchmarks

As mentioned in Chapter 8, *baselines* and *benchmarks* are critical to ensuring a campaign or program is being tracked and mid-course corrections are being made when necessary and that the campaign or program is on phase and on target. They are equally important in the evaluation phase. The *final* benchmark provides the data for the final outcomes that are then analyzed against the baseline and objectives. Which benchmarks were achieved and to what degree as well as which benchmarks fell short of expectations provides an evaluation of whether the campaign's objectives have been met and illuminates areas for improvement.

As Michaelson et al. (2013, p. 17) explain:

In general the communication outcomes will center on business objectives dealing with measurable audience relationships with the company, impact on audience attitudes, beliefs, values, and intended behavior (to include actual behavior), and demonstrable return on investment in the communication campaign.

In general, the same research methodologies used to establish the baseline are used to measure the benchmarks, and thus the objectives. The data on relationships should show changes in (1) stakeholder awareness, (2) knowledge, (3) interest, and (4) relevance. The data on attitudes, beliefs, values, and behavior should demonstrate stakeholder changes in perception, as well as stakeholder willingness to (1) recommend, (2) change, (3) purchase, (4) remain loyal, and (5) act on behalf of organization if asked. One should measure the communication outcomes and correlate them with actual business outcomes such as changes in sales, financial performance, relationship or reputation perceptions, willingness to take action, and so forth to calculate ROI (more on that later).

These data should then be compared with the campaign's objectives. This final comparative analysis is the actual measure of whether or not objectives have been met. This is not the time to be shy; if an objective was not met, everyone needs to acknowledge that fact and examine when, where, and by how much the objective was missed, which will help determine how and why it *was* missed. This investigation will provide an excellent starting point for implementing the next plan. As previously mentioned, best practices consider this evaluation a beginning point for continuous improvement rather than an ending point (Michaelson and MacLeod 2007; Michaelson et al. 2013).

As a client, you should expect your firm to present you with a final campaign report, usually in written form and accompanying by an oral presentation. There are many forms for this report, but it should generally include three general sections. The first section contains an *executive summary*, a summary of the project and findings. Section two contains the *campaign specifics*, including all the metrics with tables and figures, as well as a discussion of the campaign's results compared to the original objectives. This section should also include any insights gained and recommendations for going forward. The third section includes any materials used in the formative and evaluative research (such as survey questionnaires and results, data analyses) and any special exhibits (e.g., newspaper clips, testimonials, copy of ads).

Obviously, clients ultimately want to know whether the funds they expended hiring a public relations firm actually netted results. You want to know what the *ROI* is for your campaign or program, because that is what you expect at the end of a business campaign. Public relations campaigns and programs are usually shorter than the business campaign and serve as a "mediating force" that may "alter or maintain a public's perceptions." From this perspective, public relations outcomes produce a *Return on Expectations* (ROE) (Stacks 2011, p. 21). It is these expectations that influence economic decisions and thus drives ROI. For example, a public relations campaign or program to increase positive stakeholder perceptions of a brand (ROE) should drive more purchases of that brand (ROI).

As explained by Michaelson and Stacks (2014, pp. 42–45), contemporary public relations concerns itself with "nonfinancial indicators," such as credibility, trust, reputation, relationships, and confidence as opposed to "financial indicators," such as unit sales, gross sales, and expenses (see Figure 9.1). These perceptual indicators, while social and psychological in nature, nonetheless have been shown to clearly impact the financial indicators. Public relations outcomes impact the credibility, relationship, reputation, and trust the stakeholders have in your organization (or product, service, and so forth), which results in a level of stakeholder confidence, leading to an ROE with a resulting ROI (see Figure 9.2).

Nonfinancial indicators work in conjunction with financial indicators. This is especially true when public relations is an integral part of

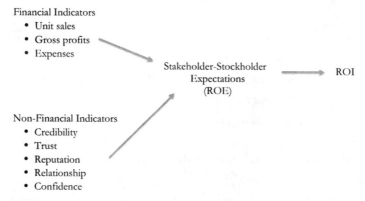

Figure 9.1 Financial and nonfinancial indicator. Used with permission of the Guilford Press

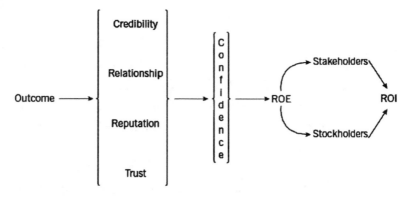

Figure 9.2 The ROE→ROI Model of public relations outcomes.
Used with permission of the Guilford Press

the mix as advocated by PRIME Research CEO Mark Weiner, in a book (2006) endorsed by the International Association of Business Communicators. As the case studies in Weiner's book show, there is a direct correlation between proactive public relations activity and sales. "In other words, good PR makes other forms of marketing more effective in a way that no other form of marketing could approach" (Weiner 2006, p. 176).

Any public relations firm worth its salt should be able to clearly demonstrate how the nonfinancial indicators influence business outcomes. As Michaelson and Stacks (2014, p. 45) point out:

> We know, for instance, that it only takes one bad analyst report on a publicly traded company to drop stock prices. Further, we know that consumer confidence in a company can drive sales, stock prices, and other business outcomes.

Depending on the nature of the campaign or program, public relations firms should be able to show clients how their stakeholder's relationship to the organization has impacted sales performance. For instance, it should be possible to see exactly how stock prices are affected by the organization's reputation or social responsibility. It has not always been this way, but public relations has matured to the point where these should be every day expectations of your firm. If you are still only getting *output* results, it may be time to search for a new firm.

Summary

As mentioned in Chapter 8, public relations is an iterative process. Therefore, evaluation of a communications campaign or plan is important not
just in determining the immediate success or failure of the campaign
or plan, but also in determining how the effort may be modified and
improved to make it even more effective in the future. Much of public
relations evaluation deals with nonfinancial indicators (credibility, trust,
reputation, relationships, and confidence), which have been shown to
clearly impact the success or failure of business objectives. Comparing the
final benchmark with the baseline and objectives, and determining which
benchmarks were achieved and to what degree as well as which benchmarks fell short, will provide an understanding of whether the campaign's
objectives have been met and illuminate areas for improvement. The purpose of the firm's final report is to provide all of the metrics with tables
and figures, as well as a discussion of the campaign's results compared to
the original objectives. It is important to remember that best practices
consider this the beginning point for continued improvement rather than
the end of effort.

   In Chapter 10, we take a detailed and updated look at how best to
judge the credibility and value of public relations efforts executed on your
behalf.

A caveat: If your firm is acting more as "counsel" than a "project manager," evaluation systems described here are not appropriate. Evaluation in that case is more of the firm's value to you and the system in
persuading and educating management. Or, if the firm is acting as
"extra hands" but your public relations department is doing the bulk
of the work, then the firm can give evaluation of the program, but the
strengths and cooperation of your public relations department with
the firm rather than the skills of the firm itself may have determined
the program's success. Finally, the best programs with the most experienced and skilled outside counsel may still not be successful and show
positive outcomes if the organization is simultaneously making public
relations missteps or in general being a bad actor.

PART III

Meeting Expectations: Measurement and Evaluation

This last part of the volume examines how firms establish success or failure. In the near past such decisions would have been made on a more qualitative basis than done today, especially since the client desires to know what the return on investment is. Today's public relations firm collects both qualitative and quantitative information (data) on *outcomes* based on *outputs* and *outtakes* specified in the work plan created with the client. These outcomes are carefully assessed against baseline(s) and benchmarks. Chapter 10 focuses on meeting the client's expectations and how evaluation of campaign success or failure is determined by whether there was significant movement from baseline measure(s) to final results and how well the campaign met benchmarks. Finally, Chapter 11 presents a review of the salient points made throughout the book.

CHAPTER 10

Meeting Client Expectations

"For years we measured our public relations firms based on 'column inches'—how much media coverage they were able to generate for our organization. We believed that this translated directly to action on behalf of our stakeholders. Awareness is important, but we need more rigorous measures now."

—VP, Public Relations, Consumer Product Company

"In the planning stage of any campaign, we establish benchmarks that we want to accomplish as part of the plan. This will tell us if we are being successful."

—VP, Communications, Higher Education

"Recently a firm tried to prove their worth by the amount of product they generated for us. It made us realize that 'product' was not the same as 'outcomes',"

—Public Relations Manager, Not-For-Profit

"Social media has really thrown a major wrench into the measurement game. Everyone is working hard to quantify social media exposure. I don't believe we have achieved a system that everyone agrees upon. Social media is nothing more than awareness-building at a very fast pace (and in many ways limited to very small groups). How does this impact the organization's goals is my question?"

—Principal, PR Firm

"Behaviors are our gold standard of measurement. We identify what we need from each stakeholder group and the intermediate behaviors we would need along the way. This is about as bottom-line as we have found."

—Director of Strategic Communication,
Manufacturing Concern

Of all the chapters in this book, this may be the one that is most important. Whether the public relations work completed on your behalf—whether it be the work of the firm you have hired or your own department's work—meets your expectations is after all how you will judge the credibility and value of public relations. Sadly, few truly understand what reasonable expectations should look like and tend to set their expectations far lower than necessary. The more expectations that include quality measurement are demanded, the more effective—and valued—public relations will be to an organization.

Understanding Public Relations Expectations

Historically, 99% of the work done by public relations is related to awareness-building for a product or service. This was traditionally done through the media, and the now discredited metric AVE (Advertising Value Equivalency) was the gold standard for measuring expectations for these types of activities. Firms would "clip count." They would gather up all the articles and mentions that were generated for the product or service and measure the number of "column inches." Then they would calculate the cost of those column inches as if they had to buy it with advertising dollars. Often, a firm would multiple this number by a certain factor, claiming that pure editorial (or third-party endorsement) had a greater impact than advertising. That would then become the "equivalency." Firms would like to say that they generated $X million of AVE on behalf of a product or service.

In addition, they would take circulation numbers or viewership and claim that the coverage obtained so many "views" or "opportunities to see" and consider it a measurement of success. This did not take into consideration who the reader was, whether there was recall as a result, or if there was any action because of article.

Clients and public relations professionals alike have wised up and are now asking the very important question of "so what"—what has all that

"The time is right to look for an alternative measurement for PR, which would be a more accurate representation of the industry we operate in."

Edelman Digital, *Friday Five*, May 24, 2013

awareness building done to further the bottom line? This has driven the profession to rethink how to evaluate its work, which in turn will most certainly help raise everyone's expectations of public relations.

The challenge is how to *measure* the profession's work, which can be long-term and subtle, in any "hard numbers" way as in marketing or sales? How do you measure the value of "reputation" and further, how reputation impacts sales? How do you measure what *does not happen* as a result of good counsel, which might have helped avoid a crisis and/or a significantly damaged reputation?

Public Relations researchers, lead heavily by the educators in the field, are looking seriously for what has been described by David Michaelson, Director of Research at Teneo, New York City, and Don Stacks, Professor of Public Relations/Corporate Communications at the University of Miami, FL, in their *PR Journal* article "Standardization in Public Relations Measurement and Evaluation" as the *"holy grail" of measurement … valid for determining the impact of public relations and research methods that will produce reliable and replicable results"* (Michaelson and Stacks 2011). The public relations profession is moving toward evaluating not only the *elements* of the work done but their *impact* on specific target audiences, such as opinion leaders, customers, and employees to name but a few. These are now labeled "outputs," "outtakes," and "outcomes."

Outputs

Outputs are the deliverables that a firm may produce for a client (Stacks and Bowen, 2013). These might range from news releases, brochures, newsletters, blogs, speeches, annual reports, strategy documents, research, white papers, and more. Outputs are the physical products that a firm promises to provide the client as part of the overall project.

These outputs can be measured simply—were they completed on time and on budget? What was the quality of the deliverable(s)? Did they adhere to the organization's strategy and personality? From a client point of view were they seen, recalled, and understood—did they meet the

> Outputs are the physical products that a firm promises to provide the client as part of the overall project.

informational objectives of the campaign or program (Michaelson and Stacks 2014; Stacks 2011).

Most of these measures are subjective and the client determines the level of satisfaction with what is being delivered. Open communication on these with the Senior Partner or Account Executive of the public relations firm on a regular basis is imperative to making sure you are getting the quality products you need in a timely fashion and within budget. Other outputs can simply be counted. How many people saw the output? How many can recall its content? How well did they understand it? These are measures of informational objectives and are the first objectives to be tested against baseline data collected prior to the campaign and against estimated benchmarks.

Outtakes

Each deliverable or set of deliverables is designed to achieve an objective in an overall strategy. The impact of the deliverables is called "outtakes." It may be to raise awareness among a stakeholder group. It may be to reinforce a predisposed attitude or opinion about an organization. It could be simply to trigger a preliminary behavior to see if the stakeholder(s) is/are ready to act when needed (or not to act when circumstances might encourage them to do so). An outtake also may take the form of *opinion leaders opining* on the client's issue, product, or image. Outtakes in this form are the messages of others who have significantly influenced target audiences in the past. Such opinion leaders may be editorial writers, bloggers, supervisors, industrial analysts, and the like. In such instances the outtake is a result of a motivational objective that employs third-party endorsers to make the client's case to the targeted audience.

Measurement is used to determine if a deliverable has accomplished the goal for which it was intended. Consider a newsletter or website—is it read and comprehended (informational objective), memorable and motivating (motivational objective)? Events or activities—were they

Each deliverable or set of deliverables is designed to achieve an objective in an overall strategy. The impact of the deliverables is called "outtakes."

successful, in terms of stakeholder attendance, did they build or reinforces relationship awareness, relationships, or lead to a different intermediate behavior going forward (behavioral objectives)? If building a social media presence—did it gain followers, did they relate it positively to the organization/service, do they use it to interact with and build a closer relationship with the organization?

Each deliverable/activity should have a purpose within the greater strategy and each should be evaluated so as to determine its effectiveness in terms of cost, execution, and contribution to the overall strategy. That is, do the goals and objectives correlate with the goals and objectives of other business functions, such as marketing, human resources, information technology? Part of the evaluation process is to ensure that strategic feedback has been provided that, in turn, allows timely changes in strategy.

Outcomes

All public relations activities should be part of an overall strategy that has specific goals and defines how those goals will be measured. Outcomes are what the plan's execution *achieves* on behalf of the organization's business goals. Evaluation of these goals should link to the financial bottom line if at all possible. As outlined in Chapter 4, the setting of, and agreement to achieving these measureable goals, is critical when laying out the Scope of Work for the firm. Outcomes may range from building awareness, expanding knowledge and understanding, increasing preference or interest, or best, moving behaviors—either changing, motivating, or reinforcing ongoing behaviors—stakeholder group by stakeholder group. Further, since much of what public relations works on is *nonfinancial* in nature the financial bottom line may be impacted by the other two bottom lines examined by businesses today: environmental practices and corporate social responsibility (CSR).

Finally, the nonfinancial outcomes can be correlated to the financial. Several examples might come to mind. As absenteeism drops, does

> Outcomes are what the plan's execution *achieves* on behalf of the organization's business goals.

productivity increase? As awareness of the importance of an issue increase, does voting behavior supporting the issue also increase (does the issue pass)? As market analyst reporting becomes more positive about the company and/or its products, do stock prices and sales increase?

Establishing Measurement Goals Takes Baselines

As we noted earlier, the biggest difficulty in measuring outcomes is the need for baseline numbers from which to measure progress. If an organization does not have baseline research on stakeholder awareness, knowledge, interest levels, preferences, and so forth, then it will be difficult to measure improvement or change. Behaviors are easier to measure but then there is always the question that they might have been stimulated anyway, even without the activities the firm performed. This does not, however, remove the need to measure outcomes. *Evaluation as part of a campaign can become your baseline for future activities and plans*; begin by focusing evaluation on outputs and outtakes and then expand to outcomes. Also, there are likely baselines resident elsewhere in your organization—from marketing or finance, for example—that can become *de facto* outcome measures.

Methodologies for Measurement

Whereas the measurement for outputs is fairly straightforward, outtake and outcome methodologies are not only more complex but can be expensive. They will utilize a sizable portion of whatever budget is set for the project at hand. But, it is the only way to fully justify what was spent and provide guidance on what to do next, what to do again, and what to eliminate in the future. Quantitative research, with sample sizes that are replicable and have reasonable margins of error, is the gold standard. Quantitative research methodologies can be completed by phone, mail, or electronically. But, some research is better than no research, so consider alternate methods if budget is a factor:

- **Dipstick studies**—where a small sampling of stakeholders are queried

- **Piggyback studies**—are others in your organization conducting research that can carry a few questions?
- **Observation**—most useful if behavior change is the goal; who acted, what did they do, did they do it in a time frame that was within the window of the campaign, what behaviors did they give, and so forth?
- **Qualitative studies** (focus groups, one-on-one studies, intercept interviews) will offer some minimal input on attitudes and beliefs and provide direction for the future.

General Areas for Measurement

What gets measured as part of the project or program depends on what you are trying to achieve. Typical evaluation objectives will focus on some or all of the following general areas:

- **Sources and Effectiveness of Communication Methods**— where stakeholders got their information, preferred sources, quality of communications, recall
- **Messaging**—level of understanding, connection with language, appeal, information
- **Perceptions**—attitudes and preferences, satisfaction and interest levels
- **Likely Actions**—both intermediate and long-term behaviors taken or anticipated
- **Barriers to Action**—what is in the way of intermediate and long-term behaviors
- **Affinities for Action**—what connections, structural or psychological, may move them toward behaviors in the future

Goal Setting for Measurement

Finally, as emphasized in Chapter 4, evaluation and the goals to be measured *must* be established and agreed upon at the beginning of any campaign. Everyone involved needs to know what outtakes and outcomes are expected, how they will be measured and how they fit into the overall scope of the project. Depending on the size of the public relations firm, research may be carried out internally—by a research department or an actual research firm created or purchased by the firm (usually in larger firms) whose sole function is to provide research based on several methodologies. If the firm does not have internal research capacity, it typically will engage outside research companies or individual researchers to prepare, collect, analyze, and evaluate the data. They will do the required and statistical testing to demonstrate campaign effectiveness and provide an evaluation of success.

Summary

In best practices, the expectations for public relations have moved far past garnering space in newspapers or on television, radio, or the Internet. Decades of effort by the top scholars and professionals in public relations have now given the field the capability of determining how such nonfinancial indicators as credibility and trust impact the organization's business objectives. One of the preeminent bodies on public relations expectations, The Institute for Public Relations Measurement Commission, continues to "better public relations through excellence in research, measurement and evaluation" (http://www.instituteforpr.org/research/commissions/measurement/). Demanding quality measurement will make your public relations efforts far more effective and valuable for the organization.

CHAPTER 11

Wrapping Up

In this book we have tried to capture the major areas of consideration for hiring, working with, and getting the most from your public relations firm. We discussed the business of public relations in the first section, went into detail on the relationship between firm and client in the second section, and focused on what firms must do to satisfy client expectations of their work. The third section focuses on how firms establish success or failure.

Just as in the public relations process itself, a client determination of the need for and selection of a public relations firm is best accomplished through asking questions . . . researching the firms available and who can do what you need, determining the Scope of Work, and assessing firm reputation. Larger companies do this through a "request for proposal" (RFP) that are advertised and submitted by firms for review. Generally, the larger firms participate in this process. Mid-sized and small or boutique firms often are chosen by word of mouth or prior experience with the firm and what it can produce. Deciding why you need a public relations firm and what you want to get out of the relationship is the first step.

A cost-benefit analysis of the factors presented in the first three chapters will aid you in selecting the best firm for the job. The specific process we outlined in Chapter 3 will be most useful in hiring your firm. Examining a firm's credentials in response to the elements outlined in that chapter will help you determine not just whether or not the firm has the necessary knowledge and *bona fides* to handle the job, but also whether they will be a good fit for your organization. We also discussed the various ways to make your public relations needs known, including the advantages and disadvantages thereof.

Deciding why you need a public relations firm and what you want to get out of the relationship is the first step.

Chapter 4 discussed all that is entailed in defining the work and developing the document that outlines how the relationship will proceed and what will be accomplished. As we pointed out throughout this book, a successful working partnership comes most easily when expectations are clearly defined from the beginning. Open and clear communication is critical, tied together with a clear Scope of Work outlining the project in detail and a Letter of Agreement, which together sets the grounds for a successful working relationship.

As we pointed out throughout this book, a successful working partnership comes most easily when expectations are clearly defined from the beginning.

While it may seem mundane, understanding the various models firms use to bill as outlined in Chapter 5 is important for a number of reasons. First and foremost, it will help you determine what the best fit is for your organization's procurement process. Second, it will help you understand exactly what you are getting for your dollar. Finally, no model is perfect so it is important to know the downside of each so as to guard against those shortcomings.

The second section of this book goes into the details of the working relationship with your firm. Chapter 6 advocated for a strategic relationship based on trust and mutual understanding with shared goals and expectations. Central to this kind of relationship is good communication, which is open and effective, and access for your firm to top management. Every public relations effort contains risk and the potential for failure. Great partnerships embrace this fact and hold both themselves and the firm accountable for the quality and success of the end product and share in the responsibility of "getting it right."

Once the work has begun the firm will be reporting on its progress. As we suggest in Chapter 7, these progress reports should be used not just to determine what the firm is doing, but as a way to build a better relationship between you and your firm. The competitive insights provided can help you and your firm determine whether or not your public relations strategy is sound and appropriate. If you are actively tracking the progress of the public relations effort, you are in a much better position to make adjustments in partnership with your firm.

Chapter 8 is intended to give you greater insight into the public relations process. One of the takeaways we hope you gain from our discussion of execution is that public relations is an iterative process and that each step overlaps with the other. Flexibility is the result of the continuous measurement and evaluation that must be embedded in the process.

Done correctly, the plan's goals and objectives constitute the criteria by which success or failure of the public relations effort is determined. As we point out in Chapter 9, best practices dictates that evaluation not be constrained simply to determining the immediate success or failure of the plan. We advocate that evaluation should also be used to determine how the effort might be modified and improved to make it even more effective in the future. We also emphasize that much of public relations evaluation deals with nonfinancial indicators (credibility, trust, reputation, relationship, and confidence), which have been shown to clearly impact the success or failure of business objectives. This chapter also contained a detailed discussion of how best to use benchmarks, baselines, and objectives in determining results.

Chapter 10 advocated for good, solid, quality measurement and increased expectations of the public relations effort. For decades, public relations professionals "knew" their efforts impacted the financial and reputational standing of an organization. Today, firms have the capability of quantifying that impact, especially in terms of the nonfinancial indicators mentioned above. As scholarship in this area matures, even more direct and detailed correlations of the impact of public relations on business objectives will be possible.

If you are actively tracking the progress of the public relations effort, you are in a much better position to make adjustments in partnership with your firm.

... much of public relations evaluation deals with nonfinancial indicators (credibility, trust, reputation, relationship, and confidence), which
have been shown to clearly impact the success or failure of business
objectives.

Based on what have covered in this volume, we hope that you have a
better understanding of the public relations firm from both a client and
a firm point of view. Perhaps the most basic concept to come from this
is that public relations is a business and one that impacts on an organization's single, double, or triple bottom line.

From the client's perspective, the firm must establish through client
and collected data baselines for the campaign's informational, motivational, and behavioral objectives. These objectives must reflect the client's
general business goals and in the end must correlate to the results of other
business functions (e.g., marketing, finance, HR).

From the firm's perspective, the client must begin the relationship
with realistic goals and objectives. The client must be clear as to what it
wants, how it *thinks* the campaign should run, and how much it is willing
to spend to get outcomes. The firm expects the client to be "up front" and
honest about concerns and to establish a two-way dialogue throughout
the campaign: asking questions, offering suggestions, and helping to evaluate the impact of the firm's outputs and outtakes throughout the campaign. Finally, the firm should expect that a client may not understand
the requirement for research, assessment, and evaluation; part of its function in this regard is to educate the client as to what it should expect from
public relations firms in general and the advantages this firm has to offer.

In general, all public relations firms should do their homework and
realize that they, too, are dependent upon their own public relations
efforts. The better firms are continually conducting public relations campaigns on their own behalf to retain and recruit clients.

References

Anglin, D. (2013, June 27). Personal communication with authors.

Barwick, B.J. (2013, July 2). Personal communication with authors.

Boehler, S., Smith, T.A., and Stier, K. (2005). "Professional Services Industry Billing Practices." Mercer Island Group, LLC. Retrieved from http://findpdf .net/reader/Professional-Service-Industry-Billing-Practices-Mercer-Island-Group.html.

Bowen, S.A., Rawlins, B., and Martin, T. (2010). *An Overview of the Public Relations Function*. New York: Business Expert Press.

Center, A., and Jackson, P. (2003). *Public Relations Practices: Managerial Case Studies and Problems*. Upper Saddle River, NJ: Prentice Hall.

Chief Marketer Staff. (2009, June 8). "Big Brands Embrace Performance-Based Pricing Agency Relationships." Chief!Marketer.com. Retrieved from http:// www.chiefmarketer.com/direct-marketing/big-brands-embrace-performance-based-pricing-agency-relationships-08062009.

Council of Public Relations Firms. (2011). "Building and Sustaining Productive Working Relationships." Retrieved from http://prfirms.org/wp-content/ uploads/2011/04/Procurement-Productive-Working-Relationships.pdf.

Croft, A.C. (2006). *Managing a Public Relations Firm for Growth and Profit*, 2nd ed. Binghampton, NY: Hayworth Press.

Deci, E.L., and Ryan, R.M. (2000). "The "What" and "Why" of Goal Pursuits: Human Needs and the Self-determination of Behavior." *Psychological Inquiry 11*, pp. 227–268.

Drucker, P. (1954). *The Practice of Management*. New York: Harper & Row.

Drucker, P. (1967). *The Effective Executive*. New York: Harper & Row. p. 143.

Drucker, P. (2003). *Peter Drucker on the Profession of Management*. Boston, MA: Harvard Business Press.

Edelman Digital. (May 24, 2013). "Friday Five." Retrieved from http://www .edelmandigital.com/2013/05/24/friday-five-reasons-to-look-beyond-advertising-value-equivalency.

Festinger, L. (1957). *A Theory of Cognitive Dissonance*. Stanford, CA: Stanford University Press.

Grunig, J., and Hunt, T. (1984). *Managing Public Relations*. Independence, KY: Cengage Learning.

Harrison, E.B., and Mühlberg, J. (2014). *Leadership Communication: How Leaders Communicate and How Communicators Lead in the Today's Global Enterprise*. New York: Business Expert Press.

Hill, J.W. (1963). *The Making of a Public Relations Man.* New York: McKay.

http://www.brainyquote.com/quotes/quotes/g/georgespa130444.html

http://www.cnis.gov.cn/wzgg/201111/P020111121513843279516.pdf

http://www.ebusiness.netsmartz.net/dedicated_resource.asp

http://www.instituteforpr.org

http://www.instituteforpr.org/ipr-measurement-commission/about/

http://www.prweek.com/us/abr2014rankings

http://www.thefreedictionary.com/advice

http://www.thefreedictionary.com/counsel

Jackson, P. (1989, February 13). *PR Reporter* 32, no. 7, p. 2.

Jackson, P. (1990a, July 30). *PR Reporter* 33, no. 30, pp. 1–3.

Jackson, P. (1990b, August 13). *PR Reporter* 33, no. 32, pp. 1–3.

Jackson, P. (1996, November 4). *PR Reporter* 39, no. 44, pp. 1–3.

Jackson, P. (1997). *PR Reporter* 40, no. 1, p. 1.

Lewis, B., III. (2013, June 27). Personal communication with authors.

Michaelson, D., and Macleod, S. 2007. "The Application of "Best Practices" in Public Relations Measurement and Evaluation Systems." *Public Relations Journal* 1, no. 1. Retrieved from www.prsa.org/prjournal/fall07.html.

Michaelson, D., and Stacks, D.W. (2011). "Standardization in Public Relations Measurement and Evaluation." *Public Relations Journal* 5, pp. 1–25.

Michaelson, D., and Stacks, D.W. (2014). *A Professional and Practitioner's Guide to Public Relations Research, Measurement, and Evaluation,* 2nd ed. New York: Business Expert Press.

Michaelson, D., Wright, D., and Stacks, D. (2013). "Evaluating Efficacy in Public Relations/Corporate Communication Programming: Towards Establishing Standards of Campaign Performance." *Public Relations Journal* 6, no. 5, pp. 1–25.

Schramm, D. (2013, July 23). Personal communication with authors.

Stacks, D.W. (2011). *Primer of Public Relations Research,* 2nd ed. New York: Guilford.

Stacks, D.W., and Bowen, S.A. (2013). "Dictionary of Public Relations Measurement and Research." Retrieved from http://www.instituteforpr.org/topics/dictionary-of-public-relations-measurement-and-research/.

Stacks, D.W., and Michaelson, D. (2009). "Exploring the Comparative Communications Effectiveness of Advertising and Public Relations: A Replication and Extension of Prior Experiments." *Public Relations Journal* 3, pp. 1–22. Retrieved from http://auth.iweb.prsa.org/xmembernet/main/pdfpull.cfm?prcfile=6D-030301.pdf.

Weiner, M. (2006). *Unleashing the Power of PR: A Contrarian's Guide to Marketing and Communication.* San Francisco, CA: Jossey-Bass.

Index

Access to management, 65–66
Advertising
  agencies, 22
  public relations/marketing vs., 4,
    13, 15
Agency(ies)
  firm vs., 60–61
  sizes of, 10–13
Allied firms, 21–22, 26
Anglin, Debbie, 71, 74
Anglin PR, 71, 74
APCO Worldwide, 19
AVE (Advertising Value
    Equivalency), 96

Barwick, Brenda Jones, 74–75
Baselines, 84, 88–91, 100
BASIC model of Communication
    Life Cycle, 80
Behavioral objectives, 80
Benchmarks, 84–85, 88–91
Billing models, 45–56, 104
  blended rate model, 47–48
  FTE model, 52–53
  hourly rate model, 46–47
  package model, 50–51
  performance-based compensation
    model, 51–52
  project billing model, 50
  retainer or "fixed fee" model, 48–49
  summary of, 53–55
  value model, 49–50
Blended rate model, 47–48, 54

Center, Allen, 77
Client expectations, meeting, 95–102
  measurement, methodologies
    for, 100–102
  general areas for, 101
  goals setting for, 101–102
  understanding public relations
    expectations, 96–97

measurement goals takes
  baselines, 100
  outcomes, 99–100
  outputs, 97–98
  outtakes, 98–99
Client–firm relationship, 59–67
  access to management, 65–66
  agency vs. firm, 60–61
  anticipating and handling risk and
    failure, 63–64
  goals and expectations, 62–63
  good communication, importance
    of, 64–65
  open and honest exchange, 64
  trust and mutual understanding,
    61–62
Communication
  importance of, 64–65
  life cycle, 4
Community relations, 20
Counsel, 61

Dipstick studies, 100
Double bottom line, 88
Drop dead date, 42
Drucker, Peter, 67, 85

Employee/internal communications,
    19–20
Evaluation, 87–92, 100, 105
  baselines and benchmarks, 88–91
  of public relations firm, 87–88
Expectations, 62–63

Face-to-face meetings, 31–32
Financial indicators, 90–91
Financial/investor relations, 21
Firms, 17–26. See also Client–firm
    relationship; Public relations
  agency vs., 60–61
  allied, 21–22
  hiring, 27–34

elements to consider in, 29
face-to-face introductory
    meetings, 31–32
ongoing counsel, 33–34
request for proposals (RFPs),
    30–31
industry specialization and,
    18–19, 26
marketing by specialty, 19–21, 26
    community relations, 20
    employee/internal
        communications, 19–20
    financial/investor relations, 21
    media relations, 20
    public affairs, 20
naming and titles, 22–23
sizes of, 10
    independent professionals,
        12–13
    large firms, 11
    medium and small firms, 11–12
structures of, 23–25
FTE model, 52–53, 55

Gantt chart, 41, 42, 82
Goals, 62–63

Hourly rate model, 46–47, 53
    benefits of, 47
    downside of, 47
Human resources, 22

Independent professionals, 12–13
Informational objectives, 79
Institute for Public Relations, 4
Institute for Public Relations
    Measurement
    Commission, 102
International Association of Business
    Communicators, 91

Jackson, Pat, 77, 79
Jackson, Patrick, 88
Jones PR, 74, 75

Key performance indicators
    (KPIs), 70

Large firms
    size of, 11
    structure of, 24
Law firms, 22
Letter of Agreement, 42, 43, 104
Lewis, Blake, 75
Lewis Public Relations, 75

Marketing
    advertising public relations vs., 4,
        13, 15
    firms, 22
Measurement, methodologies for,
    100–102
    general areas for, 101
    goal setting for, 101–102
Media relations, 20
Memorandum of Understanding,
    42–43
Michaelson, David, 80, 88, 97
Mid-size firms
    size of, 11–12
    structure of, 24
Motivational objectives, 80
Multinational public relations firm
    structure, 26
Mutual understanding, 62

Nonfinancial indicators, 90–91

Objectives, 79
Observation, 101
One-on-one interview, 72
Ongoing counsel, 33–34
Online survey, 73–74
Open and honest exchange of
    concerns, 64
Opinion leaders, 98
Organization effectiveness, 9–10
Outcomes, 99–100
Outputs, 97–98
Outtakes, 98–99
*An Overview of the Public Relations
    Function*, 78

Package model, 50–51, 55
Patton, George, 64

Performance-based compensation
    model, 51–52, 55
PERT chart, 83
Piggyback studies, 100
PRIME Research, 91
*A Professional and Practitioner's Guide
    to Public Relations Research,
    Measurement and Evaluation*,
    78, 88
Progress reports, 69–76, 104–105
    approaches to, 70–76
    information in, 69–70
Project billing model, 50, 54
Public affairs, 20
Public policy, 8
Public relations, 1
    advertising/marketing vs., 4, 13, 15
    communication objectives for, 4
    debate over what to call, 15
    firms. *See also* Firms
        elements to consider in, 29
        reasons for hiring outside, 6–7
        things discussed while talking
            to, 32–33
    practice, three broad arenas
        of, 8–10
        organization effectiveness, 9–10
        public policy, 8–9
        sales support, 8, 9
    understanding expectation of,
        96–97, 105

Qualitative studies, 100

Request for Proposals (RFPs),
    30–31, 103
    complaints about, 30
    elements included in, 30–31
Research and execution, 77–85
    evaluation, 83–85
        baseline, 84
        benchmarks, 84–85
    four-step process, 77
    implementation, 82–83
    process, 78–81
    strategy and planning, 81–82
        tactics, 81–82

Retainer or "fixed fee" model,
    48–49, 54
Return on expectations (ROE), 4,
    90, 91
Return on investment (ROI), 4, 87,
    89, 90–91
Risk and failure, anticipating and
    handling, 63–64

Sales support, 8, 9
SAXUM, 70–71
Schramm, Debbie, 70–71
Scope of Work, 35–44, 103
    approach, 38–39
    contents, 36
    deliverables, 40–41
    evaluation, 41
    goals and objectives, 39–40
    in-trouble technology, 37
    methodology, 40
    phases of work, 40
    team members, 42
    timeline and budget, 41–42
    understanding of situation, 36–38
Small firms
    size of, 11–12
    structure of, 23
"So-and-So and Associates", 12
Stacks, Don, 88, 97
Strategic communication
    planning, 77–78
Strategic partnership, 60, 61
Strategic plan, key elements in, 7–8
Strategic relationship, 104

Tactics, 81–82
"3 Ps": Publicity, Product,
    Promotion, 3
Trust, 61–62

Value model, 49–50, 54
Verizon Wireless, 75

Weiner, Mark, 91
Word-of-mouth referrals, 28–29
Working relationship, 35

OTHER TITLES IN OUR PUBLIC RELATIONS COLLECTION

Don W. Stacks and Donald K. Wright, Editors

- *An Overview of the Public Relations Function* by Shannon A. Bowen, Brad Rawlins, and Thomas Martin
- *A Practitioner's Guide to Public Relations Research, Measurement, and Evaluation* by Don Stacks and David Michaelson
- *A Professional and Practitioner's Guide to Public Relations Research, Measurement, and Evaluation, Second Edition* by Don Stacks and David Michaelson
- *Crisis Management in the Age of Social Media* by Louis Capozzi and Susan Rucci
- *Leadership Communication: How Leaders Communicate and How Communicators Lead in Today's Global Enterprise* by E. Bruce Harrison and Judith Muhlberg

Announcing the Business Expert Press Digital Library

Concise e-books business students need for classroom and research

This book can also be purchased in an e-book collection by your library as

- a one-time purchase,
- that is owned forever,
- allows for simultaneous readers,
- has no restrictions on printing, and
- can be downloaded as PDFs from within the library community.

Our digital library collections are a great solution to beat the rising cost of textbooks. E-books can be loaded into their course management systems or onto students' e-book readers.
The **Business Expert Press** digital libraries are very affordable, with no obligation to buy in future years. For more information, please visit **www.businessexpertpress.com/librarians**. To set up a trial in the United States, please email **sales@businessexpertpress.com**.

0 1341 1661554 0

CPSIA information can be obtained at www.ICGtesting.com
Printed in the USA
BVOW02s0543200315

392450BV00003B/12/P

9 781606 496640